INVENTIONS

INVENTORS & INGENIOUS IDEAS

Series Editor:
David Salariya was born in Dundee, Scotland,
where he studied illustration and printmaking. He
has illustrated a wide range of books on botanical,
historical and mythical subjects. He has designed
and created many new series of children's books for
publishers worldwide. In 1989, he established his
own publishing company, The Salariya Book
Company, Ltd. He lives in Brighton with his wife,
the illustrator Shirley Willis.

Author:
Peter Turvey is a curator in the Science Museum,
London, England, where he has worked on a wide
range of projects including the Telecommunications
and Space Galleries, and the construction of a
Victorian "calculating engine" designed by Charles
Babbage. He studied physics and astronomy at the
University of Leicester and History of Technology
at Imperial College, London. He has also worked
as a computer programmer. He is married and has
two children.

First published in 1992
by Franklin Watts

Paperback edition
published in 1994

Franklin Watts
95 Madison Avenue
New York, NY 10016

© The Salariya Book Co Ltd MCMXCII

Printed in Belgium
Cover illustration by John James

Series Editor   David Salariya
Senior Editor   Ruth Taylor
Assistant Editor Rachel Bennington

Artists   Mark Bergin
                  Bill Donohoe
                  Nick Hewetson
                  John James
                  Tony Townsend
                  Hans Wiborg-Jenssen
                  Gerald Wood

Artists
Mark Bergin, p8-9, p24-25, p30-31, p38-39; Bill
Donohoe, p22-23; Nick Hewetson, p36-37, 42-43;
John James, p4-5, p6-7, p12-13, p32-33, p34-35;
Tony Townsend, p28-29, p40-41; Hans Wiborg-
Jenssen, p14-15, p18-21; Gerald Wood, p10-11,
p16-17, p26-27.

Library of Congress Cataloging-in-Publication Data

Turvey, Peter
Inventions / by Peter Turvey.
p. cm. (Timelines)
Includes index.
Summary: Surveys inventions throughout history in
relation to the needs, skills, and technologies of the people
living at particular times.
ISBN 0-531-14308-2 (lib. bdg.)—ISBN 0-531-15713-X (pbk.)
1. Inventions - Juvenile literature (1.Inventions.)
1. Title. II.Series: Timelines(Franklin Watts,Inc.)
T48. M28 1992
609 - dc20   92-12282
                                        CIP AC

TIMELINES
INVENTIONS

INVENTORS & INGENIOUS IDEAS

Written by
PETER TURVEY

Created & Designed by
DAVID SALARIYA

FRANKLIN WATTS
New York • London • Toronto • Sydney

CONTENTS

J·E·JAMES

THE BEGINNING

THE ORIGINS OF many inventions are lost in the mists of time. More than 1.5 million years ago, early humans discovered how to use sharp stones and flints as tools and weapons. People were then able to drive off predators and hunt animals for food. Some 500,000 years ago fire was "discovered" and people learned how to tame and use fire, which gave off both light and warmth. Fire also made meat both appetizing and safe to eat (killing off parasites and bacteria). It also made it possible for people to eat many plants which would be inedible if uncooked.

△ FIRE may have been discovered by braving a natural fire and retrieving burning pieces of wood.

◁ PEOPLE discovered that the points of wooden spears could be hardened by heating them in a fire.

Barbed fishhook

△ HOW TO MAKE FIRE
1 Fire drill: Rapidly rotating the wooden "drill" causes heating.
2 Striking flints to

make sparks: Sparks can ignite dry grass.
3 Fire plow: Rubbing the wood together hard enough causes heating.

△ OIL LAMPS, burning animal fat or plant oil, with plant fiber wicks, have been used for about 20,000 years.

At first the only source of fire was naturally occurring fires, but soon people learned that friction could produce enough heat to ignite dry grass. Being able to produce fire was a great discovery.

▷ ART WAS INVENTED some 20,000 years ago. Artists used stones to draw on cave walls, and blew natural colors onto them.

◁ STONE AGE KNIVES. Flint, which can be chipped to a razor-sharp edge, was often used for such tools.

◁ DOMESTIC COWS and sheep are shown on this Sumerian relief of about 3000 B.C.

△ WHEELED CARTS, drawn by oxen or donkeys, were in use in Sumeria by 3500 B.C.

Around 12,000 years B.C. people learned how to tame animals. Perhaps dogs were tamed first. Two thousand years later goats, too, had been domesticated, providing a supply of milk, butter, cheese, meat, and hides. Then people began cultivating plants, sowing seeds and waiting for them to grow. More food could be provided now, but only by backbreaking toil.

◁ △ WRITING was invented in Sumeria about 3500 B.C., using a reed stylus to mark soft clay.

△ HORSES were first tamed about 2000 B.C., but could not be used to pull heavy loads because early harnesses could choke them. Chariots light enough to be pulled by horses were invented about 200 years later.

▽ THE SHADOOF, used by 2500 B.C., made irrigation easier.

Cities developed as a result of agriculture, as settled farmers could not flee danger, and had to band together for protection. Agriculture also meant that reliable water supplies had to be developed. Large-scale irrigation needed organization, and the first bureaucratic city-states appeared in Egypt and Sumeria (now Southern Iraq) around 5000 B.C.

Scissors

▷ SURVEYING and leveling instruments were used by Egyptians to build the pyramids.

△ LOOMS for weaving material were being used by the Egyptians by 2000 B.C.

CLASSICAL

THE ACHIEVEMENTS of Greek and Roman technologists were rarely surpassed until relatively modern times. The Greeks invented many different types of machine. Slave labor was the main source of power, so there was little incentive to develop labor-saving devices.

Greek technology was absorbed by the Romans. They were not great innovators, but they had a genius for developing inventions and for organization. Much of their skill was in the achievement of "civil" engineering, building roads, harbors and aqueducts for their empire.

△ SADDLES were developed in Asia about 400 B.C., but the Romans started using them about A.D. 400.

△ DENTURES were made by the Etruscans around 700 B.C., using human or animal teeth.

▽ ROMAN ROADS were originally built for military purposes, so that soldiers could walk easily between their forts and camps. Eventually, 50,000 miles of roads were built in the Roman Empire.

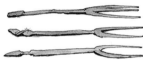

△ *Greek water clock*

△ TWO-PRONGED FORKS were invented by the Romans. Earlier "forks" had one point.

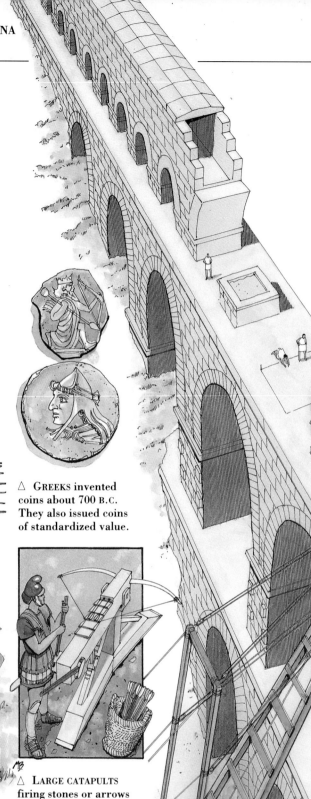

△ GREEKS invented coins about 700 B.C. They also issued coins of standardized value.

△ LARGE CATAPULTS firing stones or arrows were invented by the Greeks about 400 B.C. In 149 B.C. the city of Carthage was defended by them.

The best Roman roads were built by digging a trench with drainage ditches at either side, and putting down a layer of sand, then a layer of cement, a thicker layer of stone lumps in cement, a layer of concrete, and a top surface of stone slabs or gravel concrete, with curbstones. Roman engineers used an instrument called the *groma*, with which straight lines, rectangles, and squares could be surveyed. Roman roads were not built in straight lines regardless of terrain.

The Pont du Gard was built in 19 B.C. to carry an aqueduct supplying Nîmes in southern France. Towering almost 160 feet above the River Gardon, it carried enough water to supply every citizen of Nîmes with around 160 gallons each day.

△ WATERWHEELS were probably invented about 200 B.C., but the Romans usually used slaves or animal power.

◁ *Pont du Gard, Nîmes*

△ ROMAN CENTRAL HEATING. Flues carried heat from a single fire under the house. The floors above were usually made of tiles.

▷ THE WATER MILLS at Barbegal in France, built about A.D. 300, ground flour for a nearby city.

△ THE ARCHIMEDEAN SCREW, invented by a Greek around 250 B.C., was used by the Romans.

△ CHANG HENG'S seismoscope of around A.D. 132. Earthquake tremors opened the dragon's head and dropped a ball into one of the frogs' mouths.

MIDDLE AGES

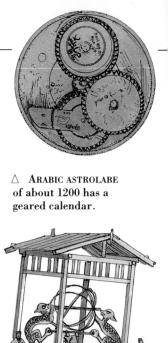

△ ARABIC ASTROLABE of about 1200 has a geared calendar.

THE MIDDLE AGES saw the spread of many new inventions as trade routes between Europe, Arabia, and China opened. The Chinese were technically advanced, and among the many innovations which may have originated in China are stirrups, paper, gunpowder, and cannons. Contact with Arab civilization gave medieval Europe Arabic numerals and algebra. Water-powered mills were used to finish cloth, hammer iron, saw wood, and make paper. Mechanical technology created an "industrial revolution" in medieval Europe.

Windmills were unknown to the Greeks and Romans, but were extensively used in the Middle Ages. The Romans had known of the wheeled plow, but it only became common after the fall of the Roman Empire, making it possible to cultivate the wet, heavy soils of Northern Europe. Medieval architects could build great cathedrals and castles, but the central organization required for large "civil" engineering projects did not exist. The Middle Ages also saw the first attempts at arms limitation - in 1139 the Church would only allow the crossbow to be used against infidels.

△ THE HOURGLASS was invented in the first century A.D. and has remained a popular timekeeper ever since.

△ EYEGLASSES were invented about 1286, and by the 1300s were being made in Italy.

△ SU SUNG'S CLOCK, of 1088, was driven by a waterwheel.

It told the time by ringing bells and showing small statues.

◁ WEIGHT-DRIVEN CLOCKS were invented in Europe about 1280. Dondi's 1364 clock also showed planet positions.

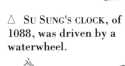

△ SCHOLARS in Europe and Arabia studied the properties of light and lenses and discovered the magic lantern.

△ LATEEN SAILS were used by the Romans, and made it easier to sail to windward.

◁ MEDIEVAL INVENTOR, from a manuscript.

▽ ARABIC NUMERALS: first described in 810.

123456789

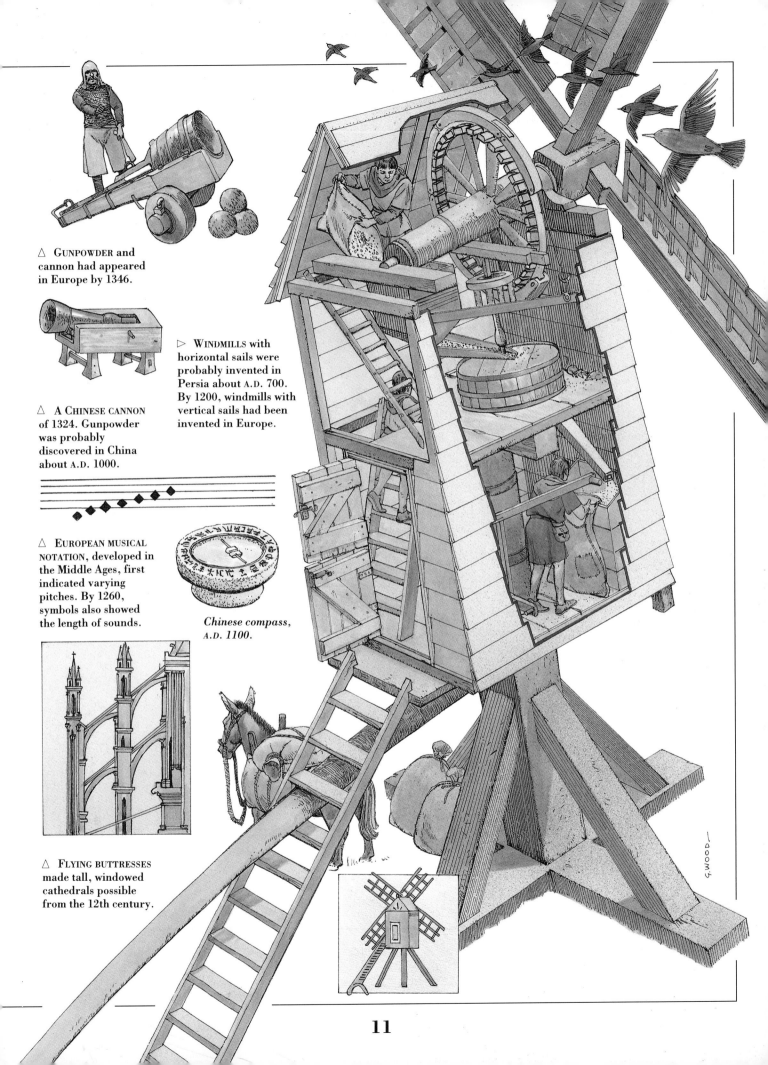

△ GUNPOWDER and cannon had appeared in Europe by 1346.

△ A CHINESE CANNON of 1324. Gunpowder was probably discovered in China about A.D. 1000.

△ EUROPEAN MUSICAL NOTATION, developed in the Middle Ages, first indicated varying pitches. By 1260, symbols also showed the length of sounds.

▷ WINDMILLS with horizontal sails were probably invented in Persia about A.D. 700. By 1200, windmills with vertical sails had been invented in Europe.

Chinese compass, A.D. 1100.

△ FLYING BUTTRESSES made tall, windowed cathedrals possible from the 12th century.

G. WOOD

THE RENAISSANCE

THE FIFTEENTH and sixteenth centuries were a time of European expansion. Printing made more knowledge available by increasing the number of books. Voyages of exploration opened up new trade routes, led to the founding of empires, and gave people a new view of the world. The compass, navigational charts, and gun-carrying sailing ships made this all possible.

△ HORSE COLLARS, invented in China around A.D. 475, and horseshoes, which had been used in Roman times, were rediscovered in Medieval Europe, allowing horses to pull heavy loads.

△ LEAD PENCILS were in use by 1565, and consisted of a stick of graphite in a holder.

▽ PRINTER'S WORKSHOP. The compositor seated on the left of this scene is assembling a page from single pieces of type.

▽ A TYPEFOUNDER holds a mold and pours molten metal into it. Each letter needed a different mold.

▽ PLAYING CARDS were used in China about A.D. 850. The four suits appeared in 1440.

These German cards date from about 1450 and were printed using wooden blocks.

▽ GUTENBERG'S TYPE imitated Gothic lettering, the style of handwriting in his day. By 1470, the Roman style of lettering had been rediscovered.

▽ PIECES OF TYPE had to be in reverse, or the letters would be printed back-to-front.

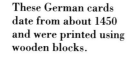
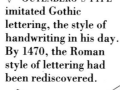

The Renaissance is the name by which this period is best known. It was a time of new ideas. Scholars realized that Greek and Roman writings need not be accepted without question, when attempts to imitate ancient technology led to new discoveries - like drawing in perspective. Inflation was also discovered during the Renaissance, when gold and silver from the New World poured into Europe. Surveying and mapmaking techniques improved as more accurate maps were needed.

▷ LEONARDO DA VINCI (1452-1519) epitomized the spirit of the Renaissance. He was a man of many talents - painter, inventor, scientist, and engineer. His manuscripts show a wealth of mechanical inventions, but they remained unpublished for centuries.

▽ THE STOCKING FRAME, a knitting machine, was invented by William Lee in 1589. Queen Elizabeth of England opposed it, as it would have made hand-knitters unemployed.

Lee took his invention to France. The women are winding and twisting silk to use in the machine.

△ A WATER-DRIVEN MINE PUMP, 1556. The need to drain deep mines stimulated an advance in European mechanical technology. The crank and connecting rod drive was invented in the 1440s. The Greeks invented pumps.

△ THE SPINNING WHEEL was invented in India and reached Europe around 1300.

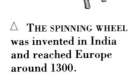

△ TOOTHBRUSHES were used by the Chinese. In Europe they were rediscovered around 1650.

▽ THE FLUSH TOILET was invented in 1594 by Sir John Harrington.

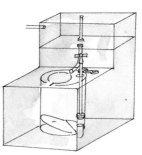

▽ TOBACCO reached Europe in the 1550s. Jean Nicot sent seeds to France in 1556.

The Chinese had been producing printed books by A.D 850, each page being printed from a separate carved wooden block. Around A.D. 1200, they experimented with "moveable type" - an individual block for each character, allowing a page of text to be built up with reusable blocks. However, the large number of Chinese characters made this impractical. Printing with moveable type was rediscovered by Johannes Gutenberg in the 1450s. His printing press was an adaptation of presses used for making paper or olive oil. By 1500, nearly 14,000 books had been printed.

▽ ARTILLERY FORTIFICATIONS were invented to protect towns against cannon.

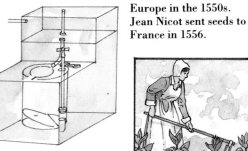

17th CENTURY

THE SEVENTEENTH CENTURY saw a revolution in science, which gave people a greater understanding of the physical world. These discoveries underpinned the technological progress of the next few centuries. The idea that natural phenomena could be explained or described by mathematical laws was the foundation of modern physics and chemistry. Seventeenth-century scientists made key discoveries. The invention of the telescope helped to show that Earth was not at the center of the universe, disproving the theories of the Greeks. Newton's work established gravitational theory, explaining how the universe operated. The French philosopher Blaise Pascal explored the possibilities of mechanical calculation.

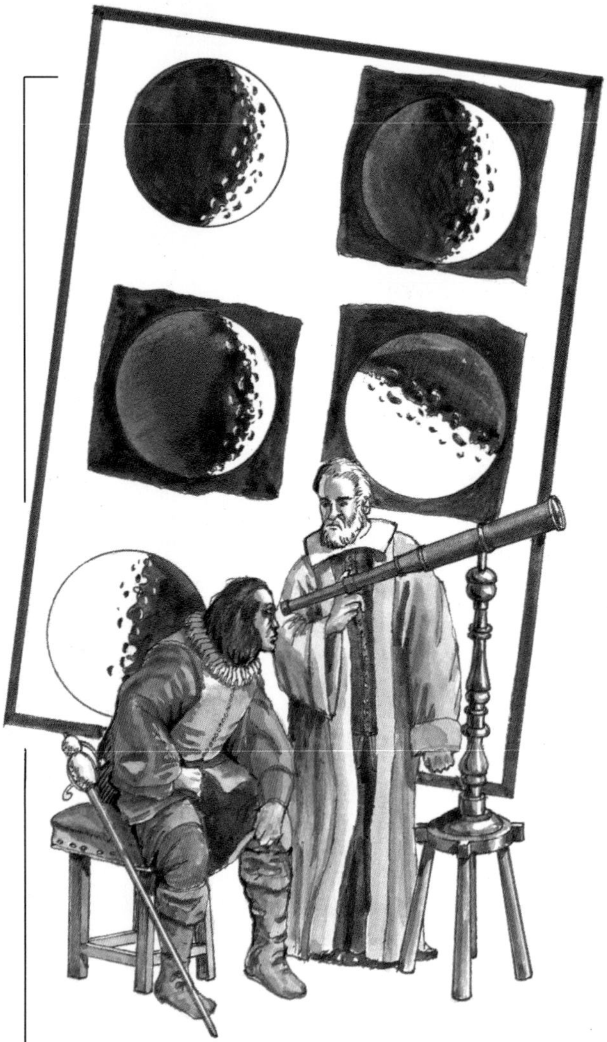

▽ BLAISE PASCAL'S calculator was invented in 1642 to help his tax-collector father, who had to make many tedious calculations.

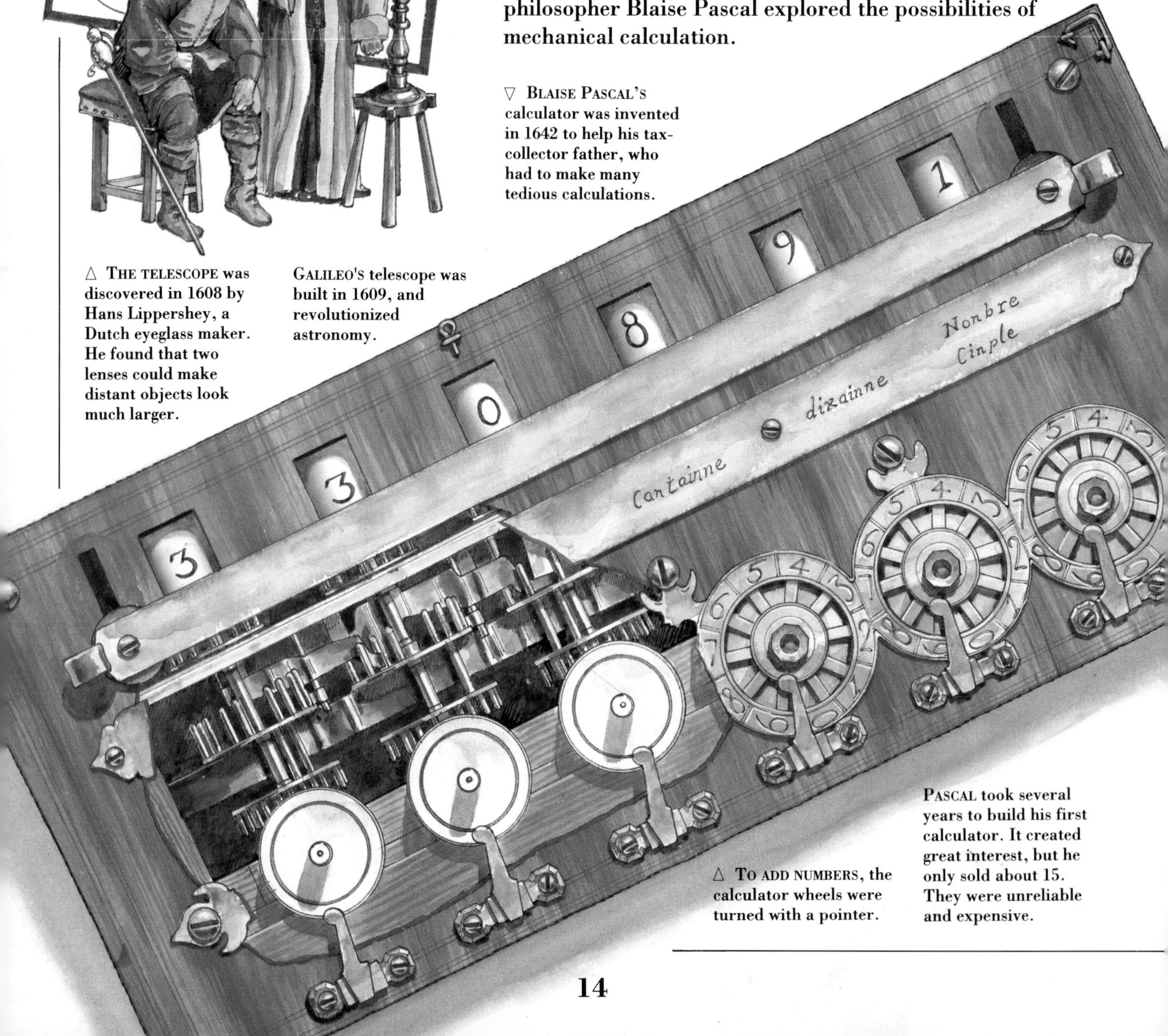

△ THE TELESCOPE was discovered in 1608 by Hans Lippershey, a Dutch eyeglass maker. He found that two lenses could make distant objects look much larger.

GALILEO'S telescope was built in 1609, and revolutionized astronomy.

Nonbre Cinple

dixainne

Cantainne

PASCAL took several years to build his first calculator. It created great interest, but he only sold about 15. They were unreliable and expensive.

△ TO ADD NUMBERS, the calculator wheels were turned with a pointer.

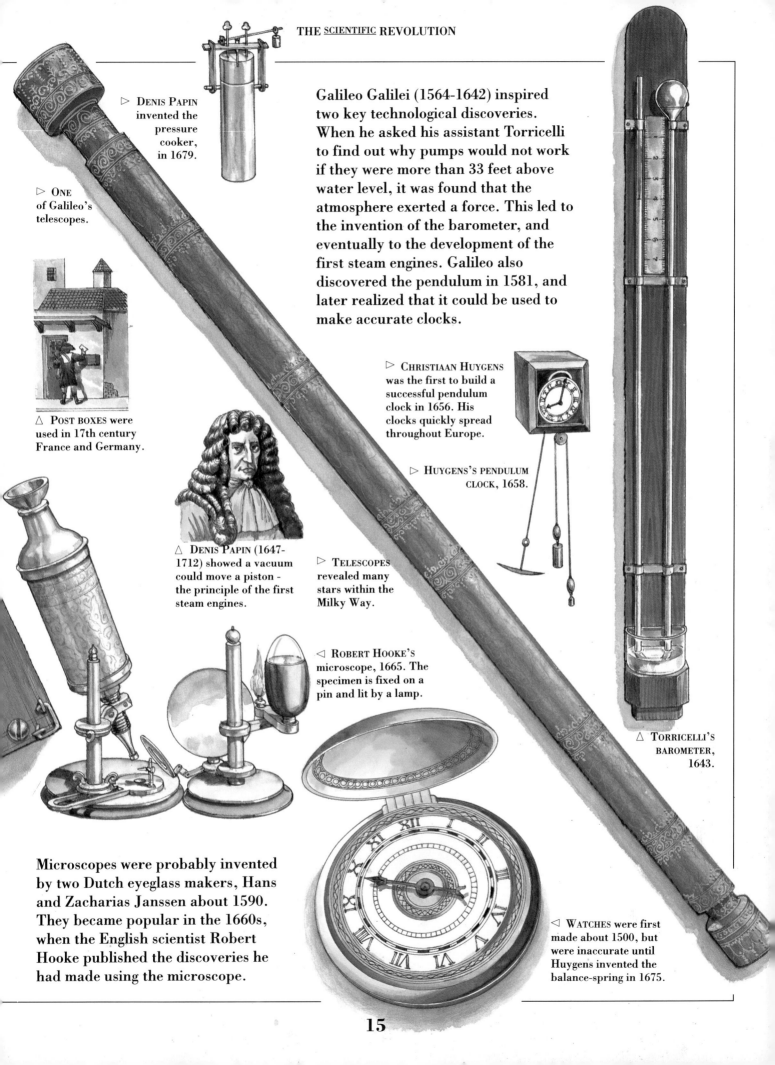

▷ DENIS PAPIN invented the pressure cooker, in 1679.

▷ ONE of Galileo's telescopes.

△ POST BOXES were used in 17th century France and Germany.

△ DENIS PAPIN (1647-1712) showed a vacuum could move a piston - the principle of the first steam engines.

Galileo Galilei (1564-1642) inspired two key technological discoveries. When he asked his assistant Torricelli to find out why pumps would not work if they were more than 33 feet above water level, it was found that the atmosphere exerted a force. This led to the invention of the barometer, and eventually to the development of the first steam engines. Galileo also discovered the pendulum in 1581, and later realized that it could be used to make accurate clocks.

▷ CHRISTIAAN HUYGENS was the first to build a successful pendulum clock in 1656. His clocks quickly spread throughout Europe.

▷ HUYGENS'S PENDULUM CLOCK, 1658.

▷ TELESCOPES revealed many stars within the Milky Way.

◁ ROBERT HOOKE'S microscope, 1665. The specimen is fixed on a pin and lit by a lamp.

△ TORRICELLI'S BAROMETER, 1643.

Microscopes were probably invented by two Dutch eyeglass makers, Hans and Zacharias Janssen about 1590. They became popular in the 1660s, when the English scientist Robert Hooke published the discoveries he had made using the microscope.

◁ WATCHES were first made about 1500, but were inaccurate until Huygens invented the balance-spring in 1675.

18th CENTURY

T HE EIGHTEENTH CENTURY saw Britain change from an agricultural society into the first industrial nation. Inventions that were to transform the world were first applied in what became known as the "Industrial Revolution" from about 1760 to 1830. This happened in Britain for a number of reasons. British society was less rigid than in other European countries, and improvements in agriculture meant that fewer people were needed to grow food, freeing a labor force for manufacturing needs.

△ ARKWRIGHT'S WATER FRAME of 1769 was the first successful cotton-spinning machine. He probably copied ideas from other inventors who were not so good at exploiting them.

△ SIR RICHARD ARKWRIGHT (1732-92) invented mechanized cotton-spinning.

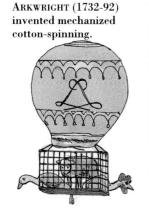

△ THE THIRD FLIGHT in a *Montgolfier* balloon, built by the Montgolfier brothers, was made in 1783. On the flight, the balloon carried a cock, a duck, and a sheep.

Transportation systems improved in the eighteenth century. More canals and better roads were built, and horse-powered railways appeared. Towards the end of the century, engineers were showing that iron could replace wood in bridges, machinery, and buildings. In America, Eli Whitney took the first steps towards the mass-production of firearms.

Machines like the water frame changed many people's lives. Because they were expensive, only wealthy manufacturers could afford them. Hand spinners working at home were forced out of work, and production became concentrated in factories.

Bedworth Woollen Mill

▽ PIERRE TRESSAQUET (1716-94) built the first properly engineered roads since the Romans.

Foundation stones were laid first, then larger stones and small stones on top.

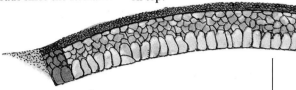

▽ THE WOOLLEN MILL at Bedworth, England, in the 1790s. A single waterwheel drove the machinery via a network of wooden shafts and gears. Spinning had been mechanized, but power looms were not common until after 1800. Most of the labor force were low-paid women and children. Spinning machines were on the first floors, and the looms on the top.

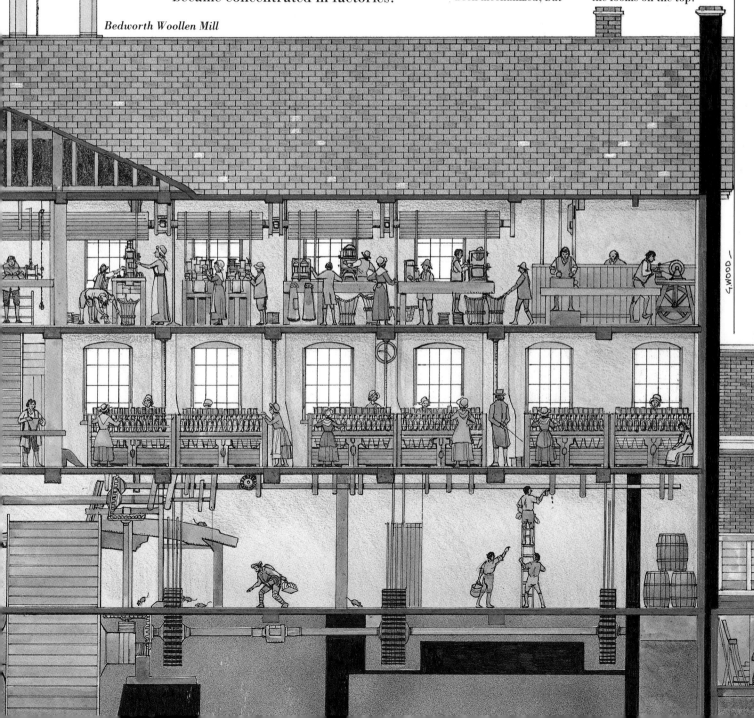

STEAM POWER

IN THE EIGHTEENTH CENTURY, a new source of power was harnessed by an English inventor, Thomas Newcomen (1663-1729) - steam.

There was a lack of water power to pump out English mines. Newcomen solved this problem by inventing the atmospheric steam engine. Papin had previously discovered that condensing steam created a vacuum, which could be harnessed using a cylinder and piston, although it is not known if Newcomen knew of Papin's work. The first recorded Newcomen engine was built in 1712, and used for pumping water out of a coal mine. By the 1730s, Newcomen engines were at work in several countries. However, they were inefficient and could only be used for pumping.

James Watt (1736-1819) solved these problems. In the 1760s he realized that Newcomen's engines were inefficient because the steam was condensed in the engine cylinder. He invented an engine with a separate condenser and in 1782 a version of this engine that could produce rotary motion. From then on factories did not have to be built where there was water power.

△ JAMES WATT'S rotative engine used steam to push a piston up as well as down.

This made it possible for the engine to turn a shaft without a jerky motion.

1 Fire.
2 Boiler.
3 Cylinder made of brass or iron (open top allows air pressure to press piston down).
4 Chain connecting piston to wooden rocking beam.
5 Wooden rocking beam.
6 Pump rods (weight pulls piston to top of cylinder after each power stroke).
7 Mine shaft.

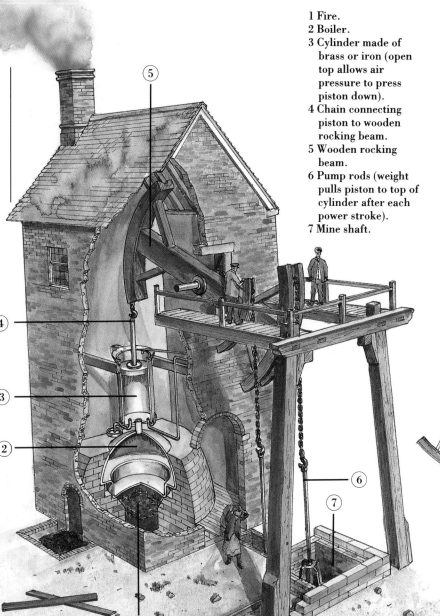

◁ THE NEWCOMEN ENGINE (1712). It produced about 5.5 horsepower, and pumped water out of a 61 ft deep shaft.

△ THE SEXTANT, invented in 1757, improved navigation.

▷ JOHN SMEATON'S Eddystone lighthouse, England, built in 1759.

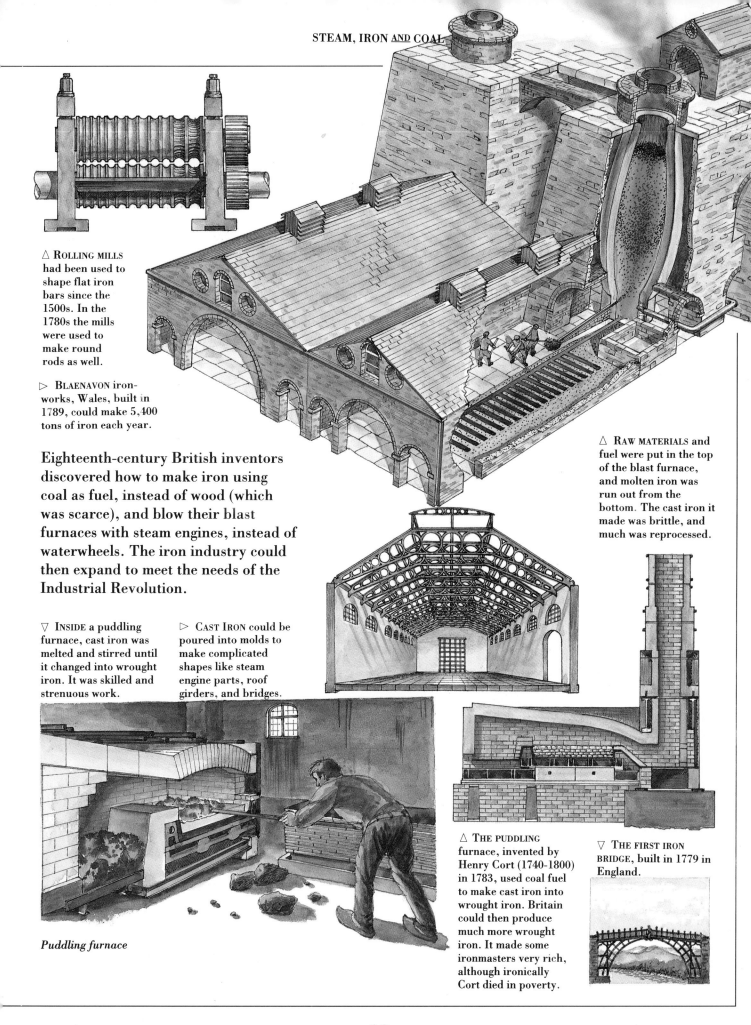

△ ROLLING MILLS had been used to shape flat iron bars since the 1500s. In the 1780s the mills were used to make round rods as well.

▷ BLAENAVON iron-works, Wales, built in 1789, could make 5,400 tons of iron each year.

Eighteenth-century British inventors discovered how to make iron using coal as fuel, instead of wood (which was scarce), and blow their blast furnaces with steam engines, instead of waterwheels. The iron industry could then expand to meet the needs of the Industrial Revolution.

▽ INSIDE a puddling furnace, cast iron was melted and stirred until it changed into wrought iron. It was skilled and strenuous work.

▷ CAST IRON could be poured into molds to make complicated shapes like steam engine parts, roof girders, and bridges.

△ RAW MATERIALS and fuel were put in the top of the blast furnace, and molten iron was run out from the bottom. The cast iron it made was brittle, and much was reprocessed.

Puddling furnace

△ THE PUDDLING furnace, invented by Henry Cort (1740-1800) in 1783, used coal fuel to make cast iron into wrought iron. Britain could then produce much more wrought iron. It made some ironmasters very rich, although ironically Cort died in poverty.

▽ THE FIRST IRON BRIDGE, built in 1779 in England.

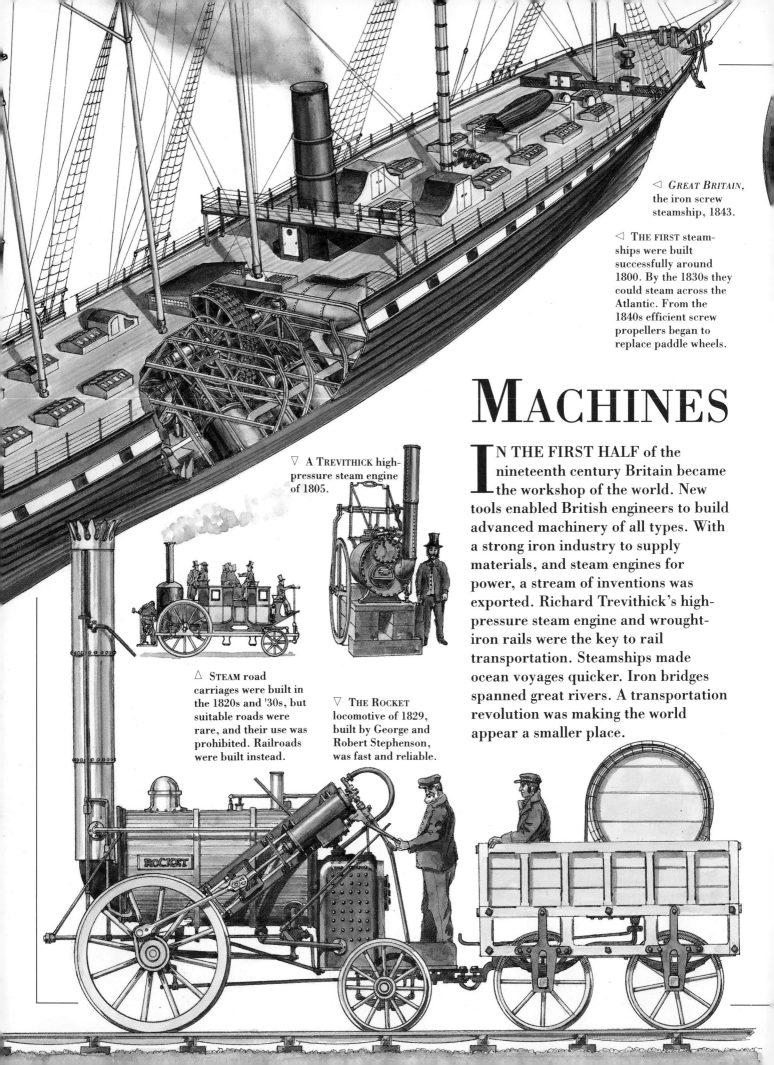

◁ *Great Britain*, the iron screw steamship, 1843.

◁ The first steamships were built successfully around 1800. By the 1830s they could steam across the Atlantic. From the 1840s efficient screw propellers began to replace paddle wheels.

MACHINES

IN THE FIRST HALF of the nineteenth century Britain became the workshop of the world. New tools enabled British engineers to build advanced machinery of all types. With a strong iron industry to supply materials, and steam engines for power, a stream of inventions was exported. Richard Trevithick's high-pressure steam engine and wrought-iron rails were the key to rail transportation. Steamships made ocean voyages quicker. Iron bridges spanned great rivers. A transportation revolution was making the world appear a smaller place.

▽ A Trevithick high-pressure steam engine of 1805.

△ Steam road carriages were built in the 1820s and '30s, but suitable roads were rare, and their use was prohibited. Railroads were built instead.

▽ The Rocket locomotive of 1829, built by George and Robert Stephenson, was fast and reliable.

ROCKET

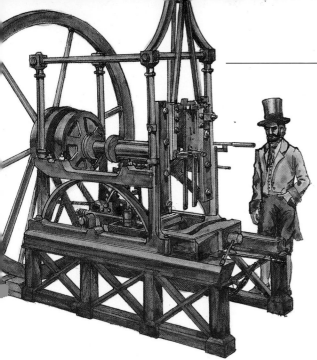

Machine tools were the key to nineteenth-century technical progress. They made screws, rods, and cylinders of a size and accuracy hitherto impossible. This increase in accuracy has continued to the present day. Skilled craftsmen were replaced by machine minders, and goods could be mass-produced.

The British navy installed the first such production line at Portsmouth Dockyard in 1803-8. Sailing ships needed thousands of wooden pulley blocks; 45 specialized machines enabled 10 unskilled men to make 130,000 blocks a year, replacing the skills of 110 blockmakers. The saving was so great that the machines paid for themselves in three years.

△ JOSEPH-MARIE JACQUARD (1752-1834) ushered in the era of automation. In 1801 he invented a loom programmed by punched cards, which could automatically weave complex patterns. Punched cards were used to control machine tools in the 1840s; later they were used to store and analyze information.

△ THE MORTISING MACHINE, from the Portsmouth block-making production line designed by Sir Marc Brunel. The machines were built by Henry Maudslay.

In the nineteenth century it became possible to make machines from interchangeable parts. Complex mechanisms could be made using machines and unskilled labor. Firearms and clocks were the first mass-produced goods.

△ TIN CANS for food were invented by Peter Durand in 1810.

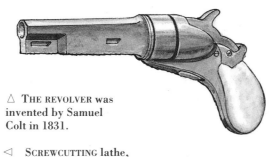

△ THE REVOLVER was invented by Samuel Colt in 1831.

◁ SCREWCUTTING lathe, built about 1840.

△ A JACQUARD loom. The punched cards are at the top.

Pressing the loom treadle moved a new card into place.

ELECTRICITY

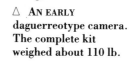

N INETEENTH-CENTURY scientists explored the properties of electricity. Inventors soon found uses for their work, for communication, power, and lighting. In 1821 Michael Faraday showed that electricity could produce rotary motion. He also made the first electric generator in 1831. His discoveries were not widely exploited until the 1870s when practical generators were developed.

△ FARADAY invented the disk generator in 1831. Previously, batteries were the only available source of electric current.

◁ EDISON'S Menlo Park laboratory, 1876. The first industrial research laboratory.

▷ EDISON'S electric light bulb (*right*) of 1879 needed more development. The problem was finding a filament that did not burn out. Edison's note book (*below*) shows the light bulb design.

△ AN EARLY daguerreotype camera. The complete kit weighed about 110 lb.

Poisonous mercury vapor was used as developer for making daguerreotypes.

▽ EDISON'S home phonograph, 1896. In 1877 Edison invented the phonograph, the first machine that could record and reproduce sound. By the 1890s it had brought in a new era in home entertainment.

THE FIRST MOVIE HOUSE was opened in 1895 by the Lumière brothers.

△ THE KINETOSCOPE by Edison, 1895. An early film viewer.

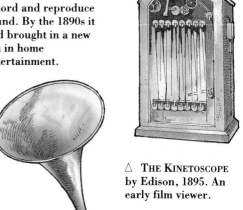

△ THOMAS EDISON (1847-1931) pioneered electric power and built the first movie camera.

In 1878 and 1879 Joseph Swan and Thomas Edison invented electric light bulbs. They were safe to use in houses, and created a demand for electric power. Edison solved the problems of mass-producing lights, developed supply systems, and built the world's first power station in 1881.

The first practical photographic process was developed by Louis Daguerre in the 1830s. Photography was difficult and time-consuming until the portable, roll-film camera was invented by George Eastman in 1889. It could be used by almost anyone.

Transmitter

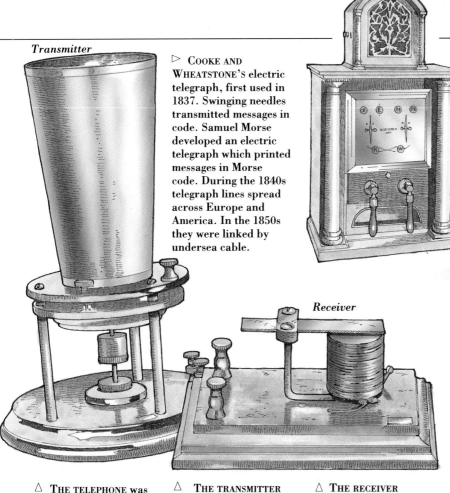

▷ COOKE AND WHEATSTONE'S electric telegraph, first used in 1837. Swinging needles transmitted messages in code. Samuel Morse developed an electric telegraph which printed messages in Morse code. During the 1840s telegraph lines spread across Europe and America. In the 1850s they were linked by undersea cable.

Receiver

△ LAYING the first undersea telegraph cable, linking Britain and France.

THE FIRST successful transatlantic cable was laid under the sea in the 1860s.

Electricity also revolutionized communications in the nineteenth century. In 1800, most messages traveled at the speed of a galloping horse or a fast sailing ship. By 1900, electric telegraphs could send messages across the globe in a few hours, trunk telephone systems were common in Europe and America, and the first radio systems were being developed.

△ THE TELEPHONE was invented by Alexander Graham Bell in 1876.

△ THE TRANSMITTER turned sound into electricity.

△ THE RECEIVER converted electricity into sound.

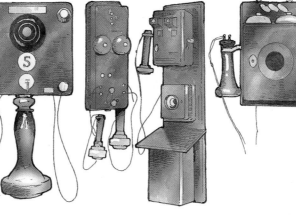

◁ TELEPHONES rapidly developed and by the 1880s began to look similar to what we know today. Networks sprang up in towns. Switchboards connected subscribers; the first automatic switchboard was invented in 1889. The same year, coin-operated telephones were invented by William Gray.

Radio communication grew out of the scientific discoveries of James Clerk Maxwell and Heinrich Hertz. Their work prompted the inventor Guglielmo Marconi to try to develop "wireless telegraphy."

◁ MARCONI'S radio transmitter of 1895. By 1899 he was sending signals across the English Channel.

▷ ANILINE DYES, discovered by William Perkin in 1856, were the first artificial colors.

URBAN LIFE

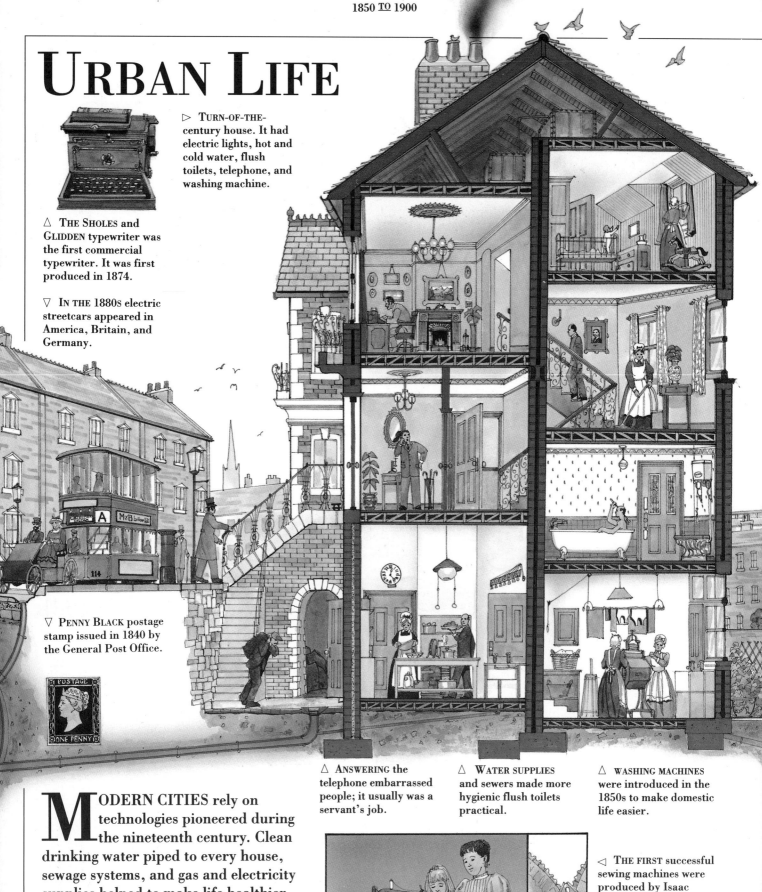

▷ TURN-OF-THE-century house. It had electric lights, hot and cold water, flush toilets, telephone, and washing machine.

△ THE SHOLES and GLIDDEN typewriter was the first commercial typewriter. It was first produced in 1874.

▽ IN THE 1880S electric streetcars appeared in America, Britain, and Germany.

▽ PENNY BLACK postage stamp issued in 1840 by the General Post Office.

△ ANSWERING the telephone embarrassed people; it usually was a servant's job.

△ WATER SUPPLIES and sewers made more hygienic flush toilets practical.

△ WASHING MACHINES were introduced in the 1850s to make domestic life easier.

MODERN CITIES rely on technologies pioneered during the nineteenth century. Clean drinking water piped to every house, sewage systems, and gas and electricity supplies helped to make life healthier and more convenient. Transportation systems made it possible for cities to grow, which created modern suburbs.

◁ THE FIRST successful sewing machines were produced by Isaac Singer in 1850.

◁ THE ZIPPER was invented in 1891 by Whitcomb Judson.

▽ VICTORIAN TOILETS were masterpieces of craft and design.

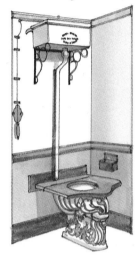

People no longer had to live close to where they worked. Mass-production made a range of complicated domestic gadgets, such as sewing machines and phonographs, available at more affordable prices. Few houses yet had electricity, but inventors had grasped its possibilities for everyday living, and by 1900 electric fans, stoves, kettles, and fires were available at a price.

The introduction of streetcars and horse-drawn buses provided transportation for town-dwellers. In the 1870s bicycles appeared in greater numbers, and for the first time people had personal mobility at reasonable cost. The first practical motor car appeared in the 1880s, but more electric cars were used in towns, where they could be recharged.

△ A WASHING MACHINE and mangle of 1897.
▷ 1880 ELECTRIC IRON.

▽ TERMINAL STATIONS, created out of iron and glass, reflected the importance that was placed on 19th-century rail transportation.

THE LIVERPOOL AND MANCHESTER railroad of 1830 was the first to link two major towns. Vast railroad networks sprang up worldwide, providing an efficient transportation system.

▽
▽ IN 1854 JOHN SNOW showed that cholera was caused by polluted water. This prompted engineers to build sewage systems for growing cities. London's main drainage system, built in the 1850s and 60s, comprised a network of five main sewers running across London, and needed four large pumping stations.

The first underground railway opened in 1863 in London. Steam locomotives were used at first, but in 1890 the first electric tube railway was built in the city of London. A complicated network of pipes, cables, and tunnels grew up under nineteenth century cities, carrying water, gas, electricity, and sewage and telephone lines.

MEDICINE

MEDICAL PROGRESS was rapid during the nineteenth century. Many of the tools developed during this period are still in use today. In the 1840s safe anesthetics were first used, banishing pain from the operating room. By 1862, Louis Pasteur had shown that many diseases were caused by germs.

△ EDWARD JENNER had been the first to use vaccination, against smallpox in 1796.

▽ BLOOD TRANSFUSIONS were often fatal until blood groups were discovered by Karl Landsteiner in 1900.

△ ROBERT KOCH in 1882 isolated the germ which causes tuberculosis.

◁ DENTURES were made from whalebone, ivory, or porcelain around 1800. The set on the bottom belonged to George Washington. The first full dentures were made about 1780.

A syringe, 1850

△ LISTER'S carbolic acid spray (disinfectant) was pumped over surgeons and patient.

△ JOSEPH LISTER (1827-1912) introduced antiseptic surgery, using disinfectant, in 1867.

From 1867 antiseptic surgery rapidly decreased deaths following operations. Pasteur's work led to the technique of vaccination (developed by Edward Jenner in 1796) being extended to other diseases such as anthrax and rabies. The organisms responsible for tetanus, tuberculosis, and diphtheria were isolated - the first step towards discovering a cure. The familiar dentist's drill appeared in the 1860s. The discovery of X rays in the 1890s gave doctors a new tool for looking inside the human body.

▽ MEDICAL INVENTIONS from 1847 to 1896:
A Stethoscope c.1855
B Medical thermometers, c.1865

C Anesthetic inhaler, 1847
D Sphygmomanometer (measuring blood pressure), c.1887

▽ OPERATING ROOM at Old St. Thomas's hospital, London, which closed in 1862, was typical of the days before modern surgery.

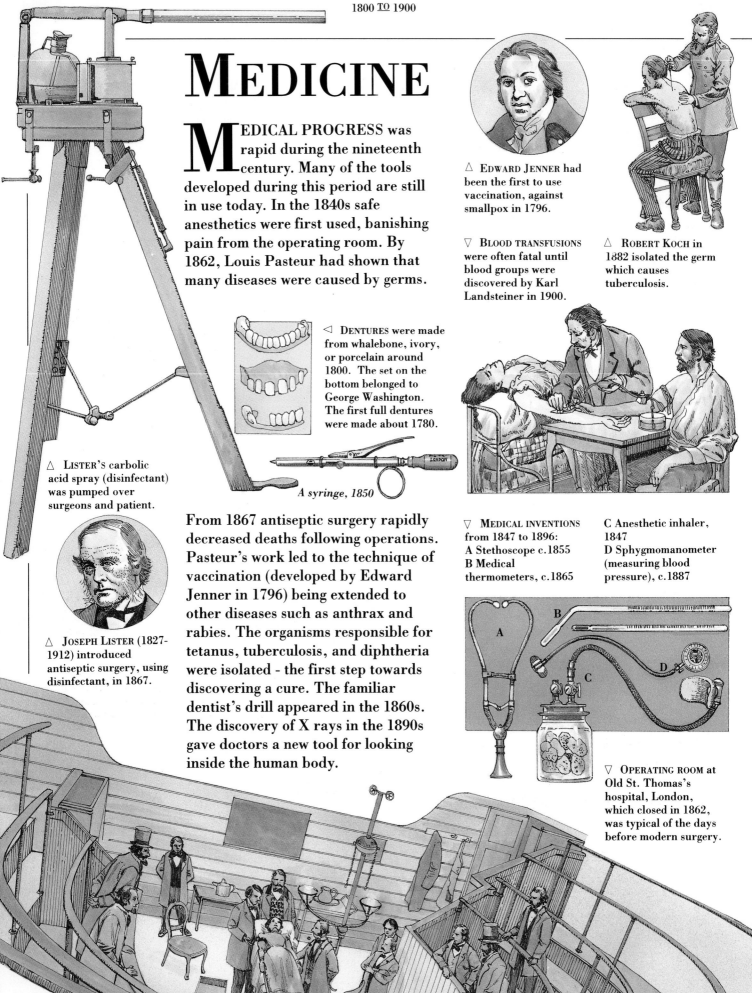

STEEL & ALUMINUM

STEEL WAS THE HARDEST and strongest metal known, but it was expensive and could only be made in small quantities until Sir Henry Bessemer invented the first bulk steelmaking process in 1856. The Siemens-Martin process followed in 1863, and engineers began to use steel on a large scale. Steel made hard-wearing railroad rails, larger ships and bridges, and long-lasting machine parts. Alloy steelmaking, pioneered by David Mushet in 1868, made it possible to develop steels for different applications.

△ IN THE BESSEMER CONVERTER, air was blown through molten iron, turning it into steel.

▽ HENRY BESSEMER (1813-98) also made inventions in sugar-processing, textiles, and glassmaking.

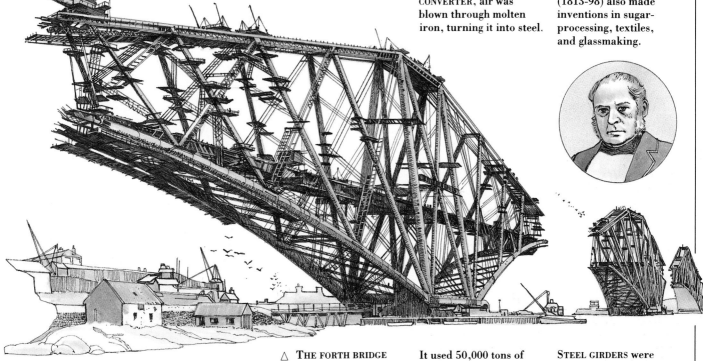

△ THE FORTH BRIDGE in Scotland, opened in 1890, was the first large steel structure.

It used 50,000 tons of steel. Steel wire made it possible to build large suspension bridges.

STEEL GIRDERS were used to build the first skyscrapers, which appeared in the 1890s.

Aluminum was light and strong, but so expensive that it was used for jewelry. In 1886 the Hall-Heroult process made cheap aluminum available. At first, few uses were found for it, but aluminum was to become vital for aircraft parts.

▷ HALL-HEROULT cells were able to use cheap electric power to extract aluminum.

◁ THE EMPEROR NAPOLEON III had his "best" cutlery made from rare aluminum.

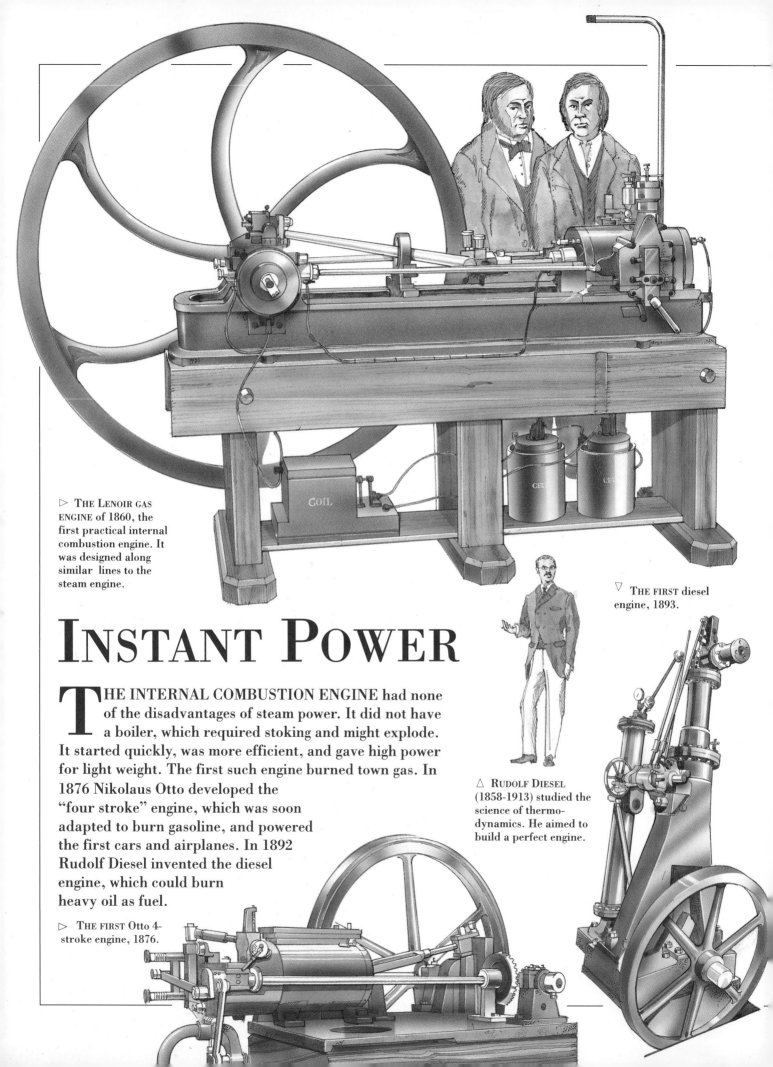

▷ THE LENOIR GAS ENGINE of 1860, the first practical internal combustion engine. It was designed along similar lines to the steam engine.

▽ THE FIRST diesel engine, 1893.

INSTANT POWER

THE INTERNAL COMBUSTION ENGINE had none of the disadvantages of steam power. It did not have a boiler, which required stoking and might explode. It started quickly, was more efficient, and gave high power for light weight. The first such engine burned town gas. In 1876 Nikolaus Otto developed the "four stroke" engine, which was soon adapted to burn gasoline, and powered the first cars and airplanes. In 1892 Rudolf Diesel invented the diesel engine, which could burn heavy oil as fuel.

△ RUDOLF DIESEL (1858-1913) studied the science of thermo-dynamics. He aimed to build a perfect engine.

▷ THE FIRST Otto 4-stroke engine, 1876.

20th CENTURY

△ THE WRIGHT
BROTHERS' *Flyer* made
the first powered flight
in 1903.

△ WILBUR (1867-1912)
AND ORVILLE WRIGHT
(1871-1948)combined
scientific talent and
mechanical genius.

▽ ELECTRIC KETTLES
were available by 1900.

THE AIRPLANE was one of the most significant inventions of the twentieth century; it was to revolutionize both transportation and warfare.

Radio communication went from strength to strength; in 1901 it spanned the Atlantic, and ship-to-shore radio ended the age-old isolation of the mariner. A new and more powerful type of steam engine, the turbine (invented in 1884 by Charles Parsons) was being rapidly adopted to generate electricity and power ships, and the automobile became a practical means of transportation.

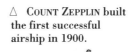

△ COUNT ZEPPLIN built
the first successful
airship in 1900.

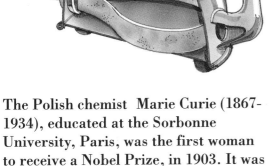

△ SUBMARINES had
been successfully
developed by 1900.

▷ THE THERMIONIC
VALVE, invented by
John Fleming in 1904,
improved receivers and
transmitters for radios.

▷ THE VACUUM
CLEANER was invented
in 1901 by Hubert
Booth. This lightweight
vacuum cleaner of 1908
was marketed and
made by W.H. Hoover.

▽ ELECTRIC TOASTERS,
first made in 1909.

▽ AN INGENIOUS
automatic tea-maker of
1904. A bell rang when
the tea was ready.

The Polish chemist Marie Curie (1867-1934), educated at the Sorbonne University, Paris, was the first woman to receive a Nobel Prize, in 1903. It was awarded for her work on radioactivity.

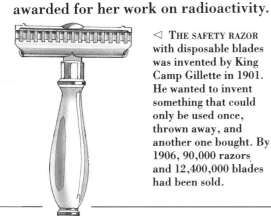

◁ THE SAFETY RAZOR
with disposable blades
was invented by King
Camp Gillette in 1901.
He wanted to invent
something that could
only be used once,
thrown away, and
another one bought. By
1906, 90,000 razors
and 12,400,000 blades
had been sold.

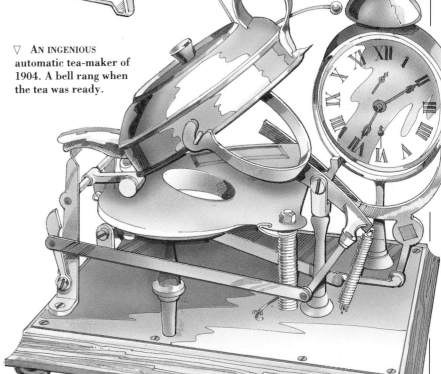

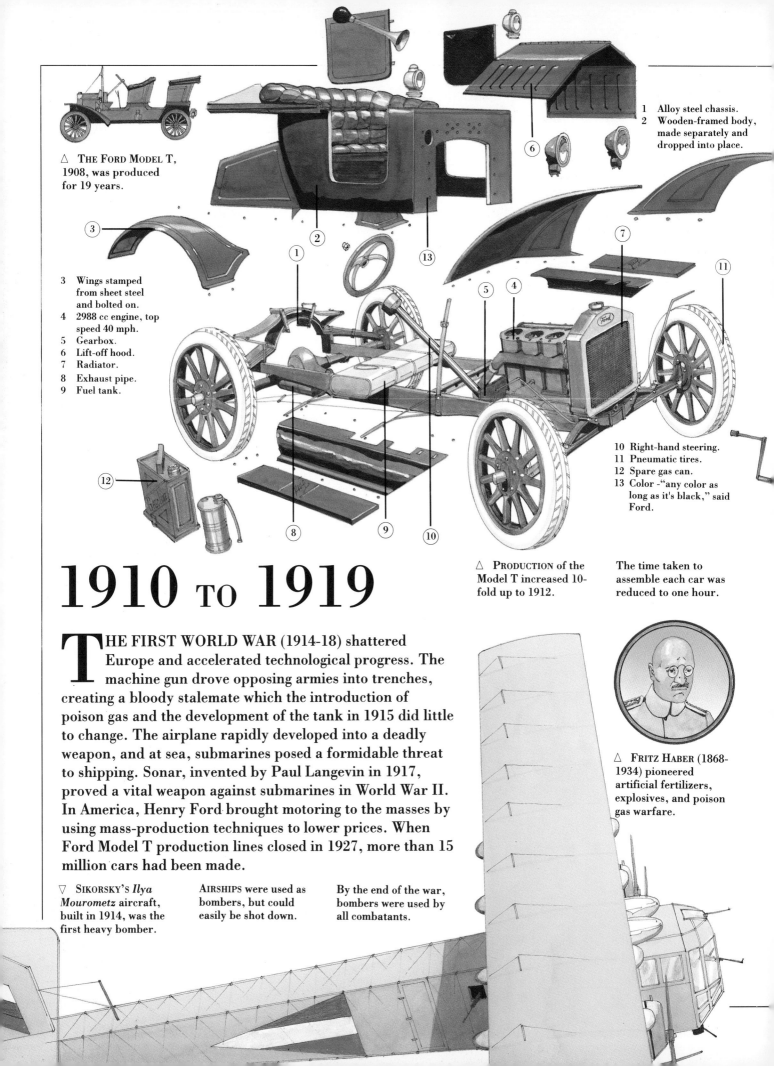

△ THE FORD MODEL T, 1908, was produced for 19 years.

1 Alloy steel chassis.
2 Wooden-framed body, made separately and dropped into place.

3 Wings stamped from sheet steel and bolted on.
4 2988 cc engine, top speed 40 mph.
5 Gearbox.
6 Lift-off hood.
7 Radiator.
8 Exhaust pipe.
9 Fuel tank.

10 Right-hand steering.
11 Pneumatic tires.
12 Spare gas can.
13 Color -"any color as long as it's black," said Ford.

1910 TO 1919

△ PRODUCTION of the Model T increased 10-fold up to 1912.

The time taken to assemble each car was reduced to one hour.

THE FIRST WORLD WAR (1914-18) shattered Europe and accelerated technological progress. The machine gun drove opposing armies into trenches, creating a bloody stalemate which the introduction of poison gas and the development of the tank in 1915 did little to change. The airplane rapidly developed into a deadly weapon, and at sea, submarines posed a formidable threat to shipping. Sonar, invented by Paul Langevin in 1917, proved a vital weapon against submarines in World War II. In America, Henry Ford brought motoring to the masses by using mass-production techniques to lower prices. When Ford Model T production lines closed in 1927, more than 15 million cars had been made.

△ FRITZ HABER (1868-1934) pioneered artificial fertilizers, explosives, and poison gas warfare.

▽ SIKORSKY'S *Ilya Mourometz* aircraft, built in 1914, was the first heavy bomber.

AIRSHIPS were used as bombers, but could easily be shot down.

By the end of the war, bombers were used by all combatants.

THE 1920S

DURING THE 1920S, speech transmission by radio (developed during World War I) made public broadcasting possible, opening up a new world of home entertainment. The first public broadcasts were made in 1920, by the Marconi Company in England and the Westinghouse Company in America. American radio stations mushroomed, but in Britain the Government would allow only one station, the BBC.

◁ ROBERT GODDARD (1882-1945) launched the first successful liquid-fuel rocket, ancestor of Germany's V2 missile and today's space launch vehicles, in 1926.

△ THE FIRST successful liquid-fuel rocket.

Electric refrigerators, hair dryers, and food mixers became available. In 1920 the word *Robot* (from the Czech for forced labor) was coined by Karel Capek. In 1921, leaded gas (now known to be a pollutant) was invented by Thomas Midgley. *The Jazz Singer (1927)* was the first all-talking film.

▽ AN "A.J.S." VALVE RADIO RECEIVER of 1923 with a S.G. Brown horn loudspeaker.

Early valve radios were very expensive, difficult to use, and needed batteries.

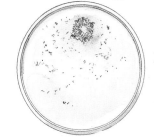

◁ FLEMING accidentally discovered *penicillin* - the first antibiotic. In the 1940s, it drastically reduced deaths from septic infections.

△ ALEXANDER FLEMING (1881-1955) noticed in 1928 that germs in a culture dish were being killed by a substance given off by a mold that had accidentally contaminated the dish.

△ A STERLING "THREEFLEX" VALVE RADIO RECEIVER, 1923. For the best signal the antenna was rotated.

▽ THE BELINOGRAPHE TELEPHOTO MACHINE, 1925. It was used to transmit black-and-white pictures through the telephone network and was the ancestor of facsimile machines.

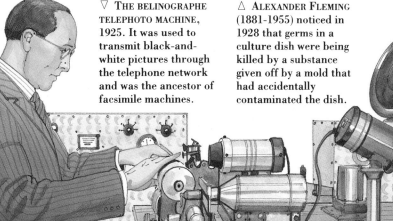

1930 TO 1939

T HE FIRST TELEVISION stations went on the air in the 1930s. This breakthrough was made possible by the invention of electronic television cameras in 1930, by Vladimir Zworkin of the Radio Corporation of America. Electronics technology also gave birth to radar, first demonstrated in 1935. It could detect aircraft and ships in all weather and at night. The radar was first used widely during World War II, when it proved to be a vital wartime asset. The foundations of the modern plastics industry were also laid in the 1930s. Nylon, the first artificial fiber, was invented in 1931. Polyethylene was discovered in 1933.

▷ A BRITISH RADAR transmitter, 1939. It provided an effective wartime defense.

△ "A FINE EXAMPLE of a modern high-definition TV set." In 1935 a skilled amateur could build one.

▽ AN EARLY BRITISH jet engine. A similar engine powered the first British jet in 1941.

◁ WALLACE CAROTHERS (1896-1935), an American, invented nylon.

△ A BRITISH *EMITRON* TV camera, 1936. Outside broadcasts were now possible.

△ THE BALLPOINT PEN was invented by Ladislao and Georg Biro in 1938. It became popular in the 1940s.

△ *KAVOR* HYDRAULIC TOOTHBRUSH of 1930 used tap water pressure to turn the brush.

▽ THE PARKING METER was invented by Carlton Magee in 1933. Below is a 1938 version of the parking meter.

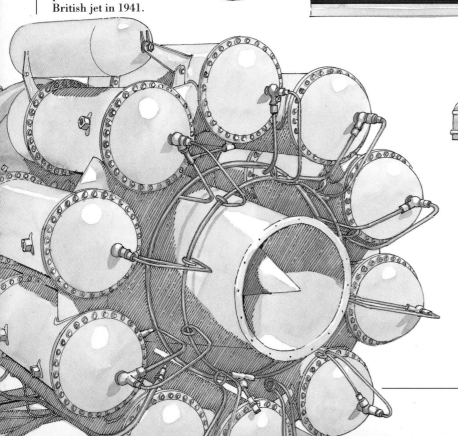

The jet engine was developed simultaneously in Britain and Germany, by Frank Whittle and Hans Von Ohain. The first jet aircraft to fly, in August 1939, was German. Jet engines could be made more powerful than piston engines.

1940 TO 1949

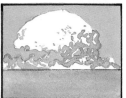

THE SECOND WORLD WAR broke out in September 1939, and the inventions that sprang from it changed the lives of everyone. New weapons of mass destruction appeared. In 1944 Germany's V2, the first long-range rocket missile, was fired at London, and in 1945 the first atomic bombs were tested and dropped on Japan. Cracking enemy codes, calculating shell trajectories, and designing the atom bomb led to the development of the first electronic computers. In 1947 the transistor was invented, which was to replace bulky and fragile electronic valves, and lead to a dramatic reduction in the size of electronic devices in the 1950s. The aqualung was invented in 1943 and the polaroid camera in 1947.

△ AMERICAN, J. OPPENHEIMER (1904–1967) was director of the atom bomb project.

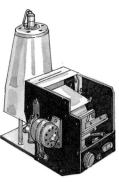

△ A 1950S TRANSISTOR, much smaller than the equivalent valve.

△ A PROTOTYPE PHOTOCOPIER, built by American Chester Carlson who invented photocopying in 1938.

◁ THE FIRST ATOMIC BOMB, detonated in 1945, was equivalent to 20,000 tons of conventional explosive.

△ ENIAC (ELECTRONIC Numerical Integrator and Computer), 1945, was the first modern electronic computer. It weighed 30 tons.

1950 TO 1959

① ② ③

IN 1957 THE SPACE AGE began when the Soviet Union launched *Sputnik-1*, the first artificial satellite. Its size and weight astonished Americans, giving proof that the Soviet Union possessed a rocket powerful enough to hurl nuclear weapons across the Atlantic. The first nuclear power stations were built, offering prospects of cheap electricity, but also capable of producing plutonium for nuclear weapons. Nuclear-powered ships and submarines were built, and both America and the Soviet Union developed the hydrogen bomb, more destructive even than the atom bomb.

1 The Soviet Union's R-7 missile launched the first *Sputniks*.
2 *Sputnik-1*, launched on October 4, 1957.
3 *Sputnik-2* was launched later in 1957, with a dog, Laika, on board.

△ ▽ FRANCIS CRICK (b. 1916) AND JAMES WATSON (b. 1928) discovered the structure of DNA.

△ OPTICAL FIBERS, invented in 1955 by Narinder Kapany, could carry light around curves. In the 1970s they were radically improving communication.

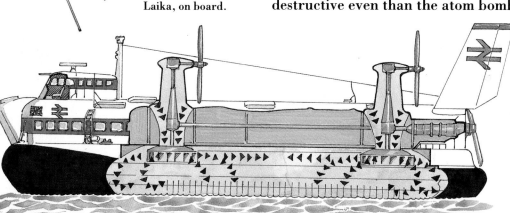

△ THE HOVERCRAFT was invented in 1955 by Christopher Cockerell. The first full-sized one was tested in May 1959.

Large car-carrying hovercraft were developed in the 1960s, and operated across the English Channel.

▽ THE CALDER HALL nuclear power station, Britain's first, opened in 1956. It was also designed to produce plutonium for nuclear weapons.

The double-helix structure of DNA (the carrier of genetic information) was revealed by Crick and Watson in 1953. Their work led to a better understanding of the nature of life.

▽ IRON LUNG used for the victims of polio. This disease caused paralysis but was virtually wiped out in some countries by the vaccine developed by Joseph Salk in 1953.

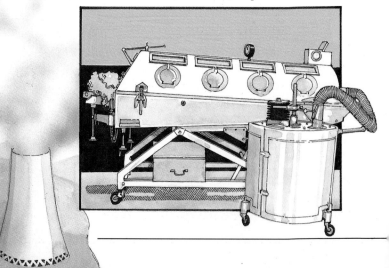

1960 TO 1969

YURI GAGARIN BECAME the first man in space on April 12, 1961; just over eight years later, Neil Armstrong was the first man to set foot on the moon. The sixties also saw the first applications satellites, observing the earth's weather, providing communications links, and spying on other countries.

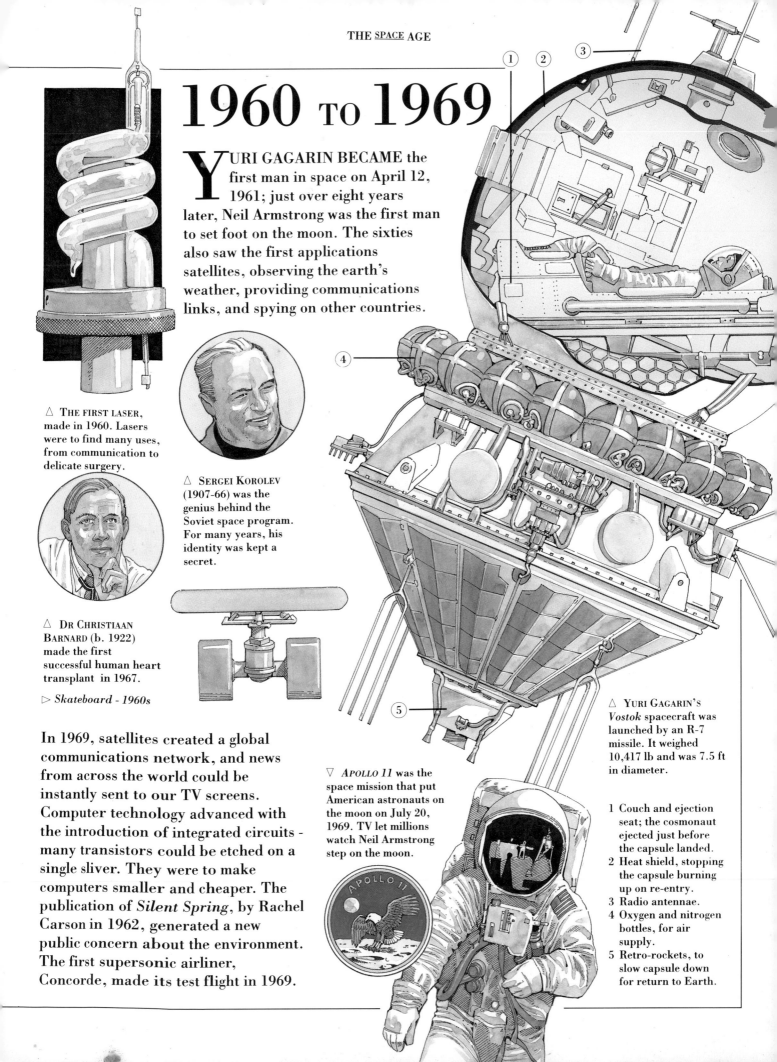

△ THE FIRST LASER, made in 1960. Lasers were to find many uses, from communication to delicate surgery.

△ SERGEI KOROLEV (1907-66) was the genius behind the Soviet space program. For many years, his identity was kept a secret.

△ DR CHRISTIAAN BARNARD (b. 1922) made the first successful human heart transplant in 1967.

▷ Skateboard - 1960s

In 1969, satellites created a global communications network, and news from across the world could be instantly sent to our TV screens. Computer technology advanced with the introduction of integrated circuits - many transistors could be etched on a single sliver. They were to make computers smaller and cheaper. The publication of *Silent Spring*, by Rachel Carson in 1962, generated a new public concern about the environment. The first supersonic airliner, Concorde, made its test flight in 1969.

▽ *APOLLO 11* was the space mission that put American astronauts on the moon on July 20, 1969. TV let millions watch Neil Armstrong step on the moon.

△ YURI GAGARIN'S *Vostok* spacecraft was launched by an R-7 missile. It weighed 10,417 lb and was 7.5 ft in diameter.

1 Couch and ejection seat; the cosmonaut ejected just before the capsule landed.
2 Heat shield, stopping the capsule burning up on re-entry.
3 Radio antennae.
4 Oxygen and nitrogen bottles, for air supply.
5 Retro-rockets, to slow capsule down for return to Earth.

THE 1970s

T HE MICROPROCESSOR, the "central processing unit" of a computer compressed into a tiny chip, appeared in 1971. The availability of cheap, miniature computing and data storage devices made it possible to build a greater range of affordable products. Pocket calculators and video games were among the first applications. By the mid-1970s, microprocessors powerful enough to run a small computer were available, and the first "personal computers" appeared.

△ CAT (Computerized Axial Tomography) x-rays sections through the body. The first CAT brain scanner was produced in 1972.

△ *PONG* (right), the first commercial video game, was invented in 1972. *Space Invaders* (left) appeared in 1978.

△ MICROPROCESSORS contain thousands of complex transistorized electronic circuits etched on silicon.

Similar "integrated circuits" were made in the 1960s. By 1970 their size had been reduced dramatically.

1 Tape cassette
2 Magnetic tape
3 Electric motor
4 Volume control
5,6 Amplifier chips
7 Motor control chip
8 Dolby sound
   system chip
9 Only two batteries
run the electronics

△ THE FIRST TEST TUBE BABY was born in 1978. Human eggs fertilized in a dish were put into the mother's womb.

△ POCKET CALCULATORS became available in 1972.

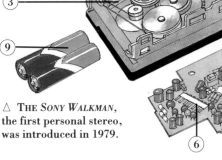

△ THE SONY WALKMAN, the first personal stereo, was introduced in 1979.

In the 1970s, the first space station, the USSR's *Salyut-I*, was launched. The American *Viking* spacecraft landed on Mars, and space probes sent back pictures of Jupiter and Saturn.

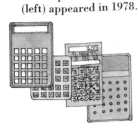

△
▽ STEVEN JOBS (b. 1955) AND STEPHEN WOZNIAK (b. 1951) founded the Apple Computer Co., and mass-produced personal computers.

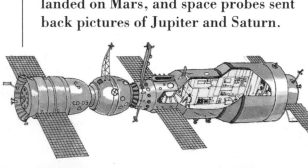

◁ *SALYUT-1* was launched in 1971, but its crew died when their capsule lost air as it returned to Earth.

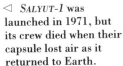

△ THE APPLE II, the first popular personal computer, appeared in 1977, costing $1,195 without accessories.

THE 1980S

THE AMERICAN SPACE SHUTTLE made its first flight in 1981. But in 1986 public confidence in complicated technologies was shattered by two dramatic accidents. The American space shuttle *Challenger* exploded soon after launch on January 28, and on April 25 a nuclear reactor at Chernobyl in the Soviet Union blew up, spreading radioactivity over Europe. Nuclear power programs in other countries were scaled down or halted. The American manned space program was grounded until 1988.

1 Crew compartment
2 Cargo bay
3 Spacelab access
   tunnel
4 Spacelab laboratory
   modules
5 Racks containing
   experiments

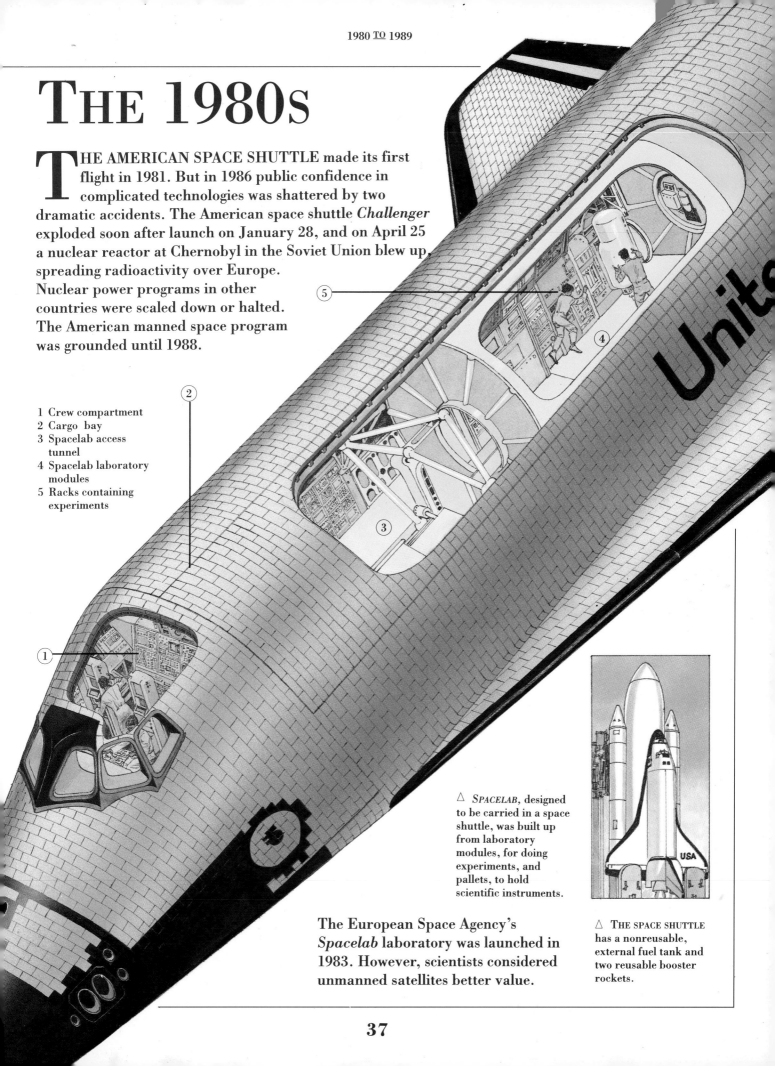

△ SPACELAB, designed to be carried in a space shuttle, was built up from laboratory modules, for doing experiments, and pallets, to hold scientific instruments.

The European Space Agency's *Spacelab* laboratory was launched in 1983. However, scientists considered unmanned satellites better value.

△ THE SPACE SHUTTLE has a nonreusable, external fuel tank and two reusable booster rockets.

HOME & WORK

DURING THE 1970s AND '80s the mass-production of smaller electronic components led to a wide range of sophisticated devices becoming commonplace. Microwave ovens, video recorders, portable telephones, and compact disks became increasingly popular. The impact of cheap computing power was felt both at home and at work. Word processors and robotic production lines also became increasingly common; "computer crime" also increased. The combination of portable video cameras and communications satellites created "electronic news gathering," where reporters could instantly beam up news, from anywhere in the world, to communications satellites.

△ COMPACT DISKS were produced in 1980, offering an alternative to scratchable records.

▽ HIGH-DEFINITION television systems were developed in the 1980s. The first experimental live broadcast was in 1990. HDTV systems offer clearer pictures and stereo sound.

△ MICROWAVE OVENS, popular in the 1970s, use a beam of high-energy radio waves.

◁ DIGITAL AUDIO TAPE RECORDERS, introduced in 1987, increased the quality of recording.

△ CAMCORDERS (video cameras/recorders) became more popular after the smaller and lighter *Video 8* system was introduced in 1985.

▽ A MODERN ROBOT car production line uses varying robots, each programmed for a different job.

1 Welding robots work on each car body.
2 Suspension holes are drilled by another type of robot.

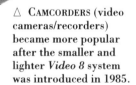

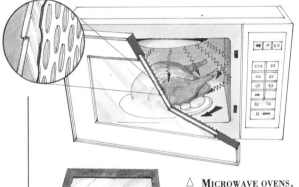

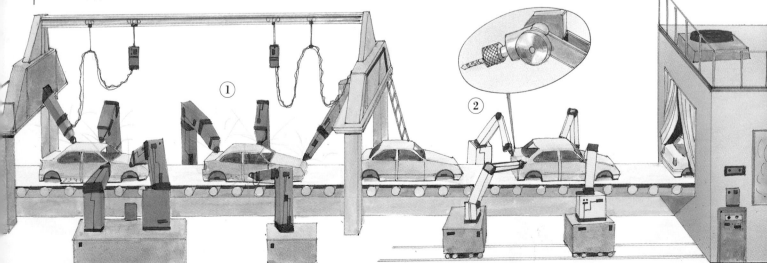

Further increases in the power of microprocessors enabled sophisticated industrial robots to be produced. In the late 1970s robots were being used to weld car bodies and to spray them with paint. By 1980, more versatile robots had been developed, which could carry out simple assembly tasks such as tightening nuts, and robot assembly lines became possible.

▷ THE PHOTOCOPIER uses an electrically charged drum to photograph a document, instead of a film. Light alters the pattern of electric charge on the drum, making an invisible negative of the document. The picture is revealed by spraying the drum with toner powder attracted to the charged areas. A sheet of paper is then passed under the drum, picking up the toner. Heater rollers bond the toner to the paper.

◁ PERSONAL COMPUTERS began to replace typewriters in the 1980s, when word processing programs became available. They could also be used to play video games or produce complex diagrams using graphics programs. They were capable of operating machine tools, mass-producing complex parts.

△ PORTABLE PHONES - a 1980s status symbol.

▽ FACSIMILE MACHINES use microprocessors.

Portable telephones became commonplace in the 1980s. Cellular radio networks (first used in America and Japan in the late 1970s) allowed people to make phone calls almost anywhere. Facsimile machines were not common until international standards were established in the late 1970s, making different makes of the "fax" machine compatible.

3 Robots install electric components.

4 These robots have delicate mechanical fingers.

5 Robots use suckers to fit glass.

6 Robots with flexible grippers install the engines.

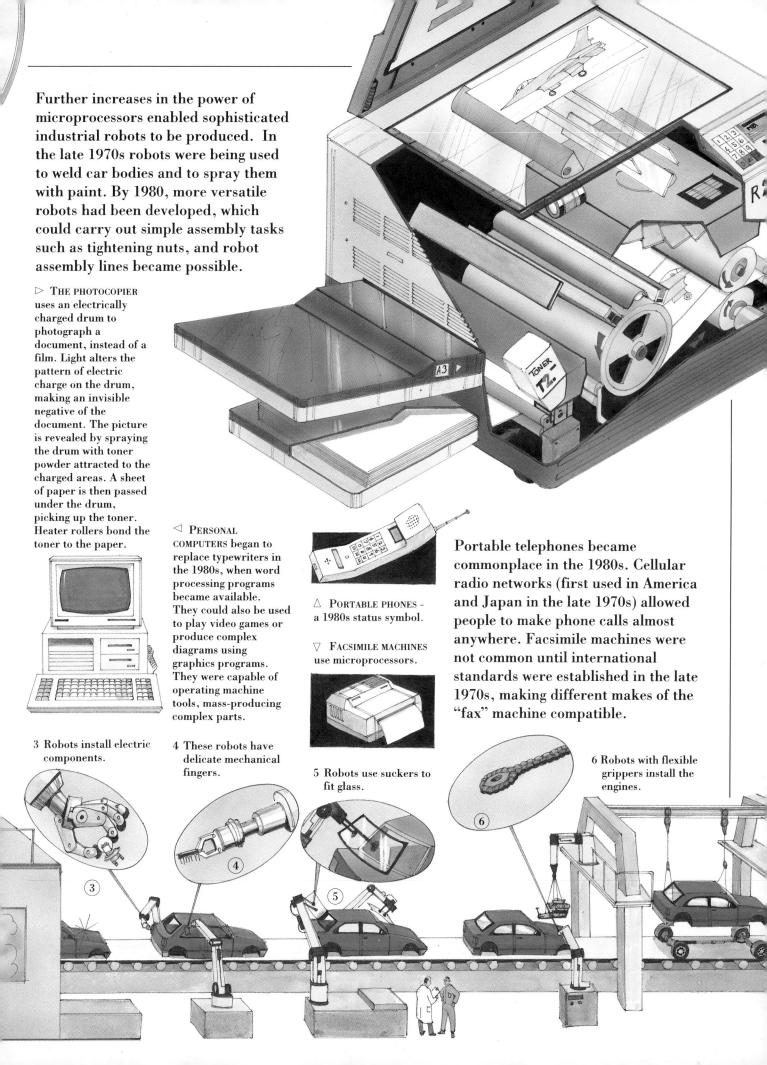

BIOTECHNOLOGY

▷ THE ONCOMOUSE, created using genetic engineering techniques, was the first patented animal. It was designed for cancer research.

Oncomouse

△ THE FIRST 30 HOURS of an embryo. After the egg is fertilized by the sperm, the egg and sperm fuse, and the cell begins to divide.

BIOTECHNOLOGY is the use of living organisms to create products, manage the environment, or control industrial processes. The use of such processes goes back to 6000 B.C. when yeast was first used to ferment beer. Bread, cheese, and wine are other traditional biotechnological products. From the 1940s the new science of molecular biology laid the foundations for what we call biotechnology.

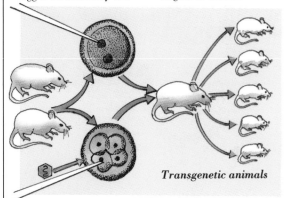

Transgenetic animals

◁ TRANSGENETIC ANIMALS were first produced in 1981 and contain genetic information carried in DNA from other species. They are created by removing a fertilized egg, injecting DNA, and replacing the egg. The first such animals were given a gene for growth, and grew up to 50% larger than normal mice.

▷ MANY FAMILIAR FOODSTUFFS are products of what we now call biotechnology.

The discovery of recombinant DNA by Hamilton Smith and Daniel Nathans in 1970 raised the possibility of genetic engineering. They discovered how to cut out fragments of DNA information and then recombine them to build a new DNA. In the future, genetic defects might be "edited-out," or new characteristics put in by such means. Such research also led to a new identification technique, DNA fingerprinting.

△ IN THE 1960s Dr. Norman Borlaug made a "green revolution" by selectively breeding more productive crops.

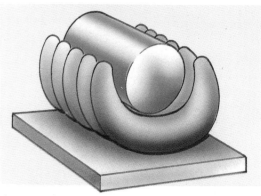

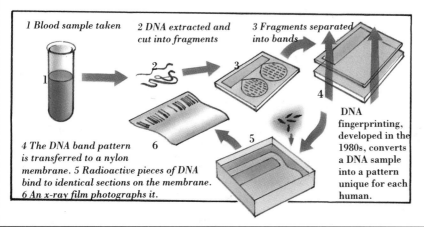

1 Blood sample taken 2 DNA extracted and cut into fragments 3 Fragments separated into bands

DNA fingerprinting, developed in the 1980s, converts a DNA sample into a pattern unique for each human.

4 The DNA band pattern is transferred to a nylon membrane. 5 Radioactive pieces of DNA bind to identical sections on the membrane. 6 An x-ray film photographs it.

△ BIOCHIPS - integrated circuits grown from living material may, one day, be made by bio-technologists. Such "chips" could create a revolution in electronics. They could assemble themselves by growing into place, and may implant into the human body.

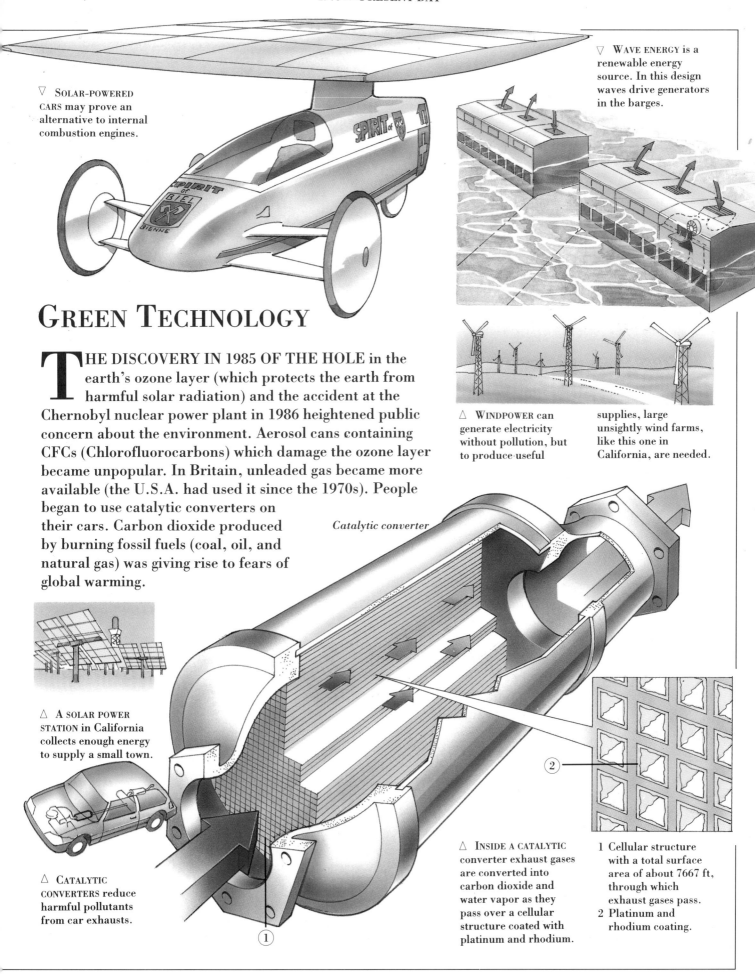

▽ SOLAR-POWERED CARS may prove an alternative to internal combustion engines.

▽ WAVE ENERGY is a renewable energy source. In this design waves drive generators in the barges.

GREEN TECHNOLOGY

THE DISCOVERY IN 1985 OF THE HOLE in the earth's ozone layer (which protects the earth from harmful solar radiation) and the accident at the Chernobyl nuclear power plant in 1986 heightened public concern about the environment. Aerosol cans containing CFCs (Chlorofluorocarbons) which damage the ozone layer became unpopular. In Britain, unleaded gas became more available (the U.S.A. had used it since the 1970s). People began to use catalytic converters on their cars. Carbon dioxide produced by burning fossil fuels (coal, oil, and natural gas) was giving rise to fears of global warming.

△ WINDPOWER can generate electricity without pollution, but to produce useful supplies, large unsightly wind farms, like this one in California, are needed.

Catalytic converter

△ A SOLAR POWER STATION in California collects enough energy to supply a small town.

△ CATALYTIC CONVERTERS reduce harmful pollutants from car exhausts.

①

△ INSIDE A CATALYTIC converter exhaust gases are converted into carbon dioxide and water vapor as they pass over a cellular structure coated with platinum and rhodium.

②

1 Cellular structure with a total surface area of about 7667 ft, through which exhaust gases pass.
2 Platinum and rhodium coating.

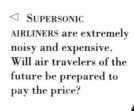

THE FUTURE

PREDICTING THE FUTURE is a chancy business. Science fiction authors wrote of computerized futures, but none predicted the personal computer. Predictions of the first moon landing abounded long before the event, but nobody foresaw that millions would watch it live on their televisions. Conditions in the future will be dictated by environmental concerns. Changes in the earth's climate caused by global warming or the ozone hole could radically alter people's perceptions of technology. Oil, coal, and natural gas will become scarcer and environmental damage will become greater.

◁ SUPERSONIC AIRLINERS are extremely noisy and expensive. Will air travelers of the future be prepared to pay the price?

△ DEVELOPMENT of larger magnetic levitation trains was underway in the 1980s.

People may find the automobile an expensive luxury, polluting the atmosphere and congesting cities. Magnetic levitation trains could provide high-speed transportation. Computer and communications technology may allow people to work from home. Virtual reality systems could make it unnecessary to leave home to sample entertainment.

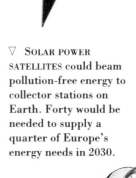

▽ SOLAR POWER SATELLITES could beam pollution-free energy to collector stations on Earth. Forty would be needed to supply a quarter of Europe's energy needs in 2030.

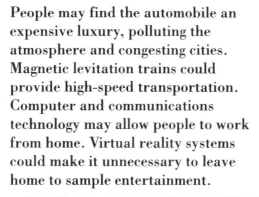

△ VIRTUAL REALITY arcade games were introduced in 1991. Video helmets take players to a world of sound and pictures.

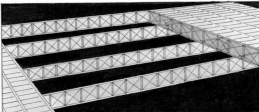

▽ OFFSHORE AIRPORTS might be built near intelligent cities, where services would be computer controlled.

The boundary between air travel and spaceflight may be blurred by aerospace planes, capable of flying continent-to-continent, or on to a space station. To serve such aircraft, offshore airports may be built. Space travel might be abandoned in the future as too costly, or bases established on the moon.

△ SPACE SHUTTLES may be built by other nations. "Single-stage to orbit" spacecraft would fly into space from airport runways and reduce the cost of getting into space.

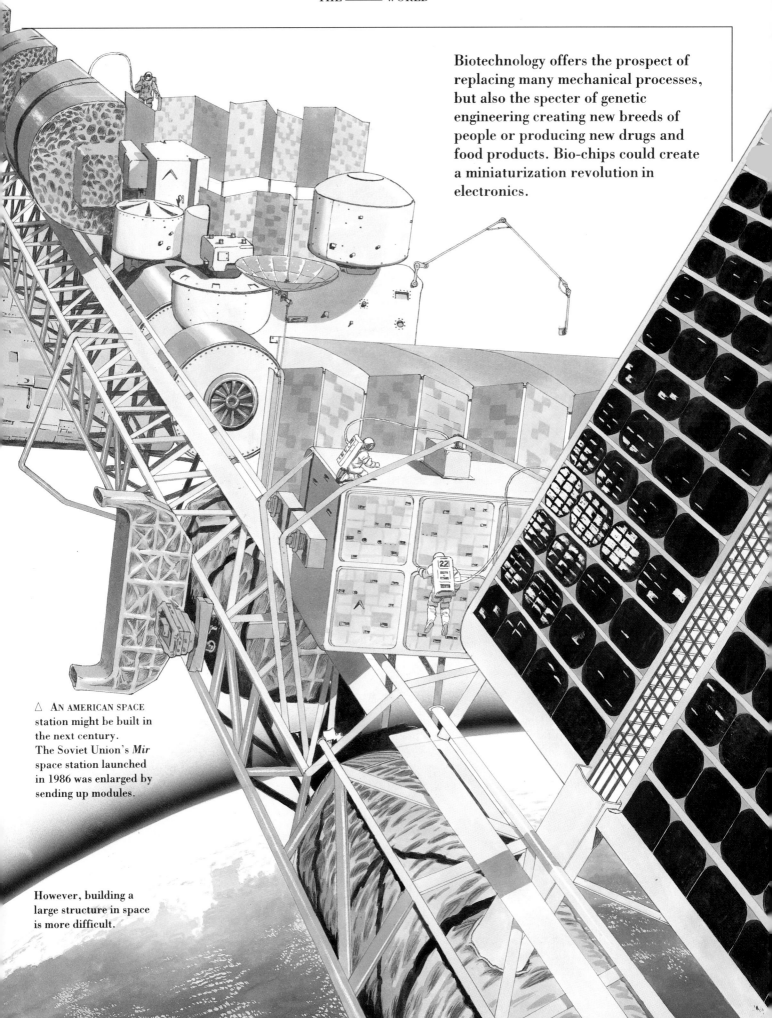

Biotechnology offers the prospect of replacing many mechanical processes, but also the specter of genetic engineering creating new breeds of people or producing new drugs and food products. Bio-chips could create a miniaturization revolution in electronics.

△ AN AMERICAN SPACE station might be built in the next century. The Soviet Union's *Mir* space station launched in 1986 was enlarged by sending up modules.

However, building a large structure in space is more difficult.

Timeline

Fire.
500,000 B.C.

B.C.
2,000,000 *Homo habilis* (able man) appears and learns to use stone knives as tools and weapons.
500,000 Fire tamed by a new human species, *Homo erectus*.
200,000 *Homo erectus* evolves into Neanderthal man.
50,000 *Homo sapiens* (modern man) appears.
c.20,000 Invention of the bow and arrow.

Sumerian wheeled carts, 3000 B.C.

12,000 Domestication of animals begins.
8000 Agriculture invented.
7000 Pottery. Discovery that heated pots are hard and durable. The potter's wheel, an early use of rotary motion.
6000 Weaving.
5000 Irrigation systems developed in the Middle East.

Seismoscope, A.D. 132

4000 First use of metals - copper smelted for making ornaments and tools.

3600 Bronze, a hard copper tin alloy, discovered and used for making weapons, tools and armor.
3500 Wheeled carts appear and writing invented in Sumeria.
2800 The Egyptians devise the 12-month, 365-day calendar, used for predicting flooding of the Nile.
1550 Earliest surviving medical textbook written in Egypt.
1400 Steel produced.
1100 Iron Age starts.
700 The first purpose-made sundials appear.
650 Standardized coins used by Greeks.

512 The Chinese produce cast iron from blast furnaces.
510 A Greek produces the earliest surviving world map.
400 The Greeks invent the catapult, the first artillery weapon.
312 Work begins on the Appian Way, the first great Roman road.
210 Archimedes, the Greek scientist, invents the Archimedean screw for raising water, and works out the theory of levers.
100 Glassblowing invented in Syria.
A.D.
100 Paper invented in China by Tsai Lun.
300 Stirrups invented in China, enabling horse-riders to use swords and spears effectively.
475 The horse collar invented in China.

600 The heavy plow invented by the Slavs.
770 Horseshoes come into use in Europe.
810 First description of Arabic numerals.
1000 The Chinese (Sung Dynasty) discover a weak form of gunpowder.
1060 Earliest reference to a water-powered fulling mill for finishing cloth.
1100 Water power used for ironmaking in Europe.
1137 Completion of the Abbey of St. Denis, France, the first large-scale use of flying buttresses.
1180 Windmills in Europe. Properties of the compass known in Europe.
1249 Roger Bacon gives earliest European recipe for gunpowder.
1286 Eyeglasses are invented in Europe.
1291 The Venetian glass industry producing mirrors.
1300 Spinning wheels found in Europe. Distilled liquors first made by the alchemist Arnau de Villanova.
1335 The earliest recorded mechanical clock is built in Italy.
1400 Earliest European blast furnaces built to make cast iron.
1436 The Italian artist Leon Battista Alberti describes perspective drawing.
1454 Johannes Gutenberg begins the Gutenberg Bible, the first European book printed.
c.1500 The first watches are made.
1543 Nicholas Copernicus's heliocentric theory suggests the earth is not the center of the universe.

1556 Agricola's book describes waterwheel-driven mine pumps and hoists.
1568 Mercator invents the Mercator projection for maps of the world.
1581 Galileo Galilei discovers the pendulum.
1589 Edmund Lee invents the stocking frame, allowing a single knitter to outproduce hand knitters.
c.1590 The Janssen brothers invent the microscope.
1592 Galileo devises the first thermometer.
1608 Hans Lippershey invents the telescope.
1609 Galileo uses a telescope to look at the the night sky, and makes revolutionary astronomical discoveries.

Leonardo da Vinci

c.1620 The first stage coaches appear.
1642 Blaise Pascal invents one of the first mechanical calculators.
1643 Galileo's assistant, Torricelli, invents the barometer.
1656 Christiaan Huygens's pendulum clock improve time-keeping.

1665 Robert Hooke describes the cellular structure of cork, discovered using a microscope.
1675 Huygens improves the timekeeping of watches, by inventing the spiral balance spring.
1676 Antoni Van Leeuwenhoek discovers microorganisms using a powerful microscope.
1687 Isaac Newton publishes the *Principia*, describing the laws of gravity.
1698 Savery patents an impractical form of steam pump, but starts people thinking about the possibility of steam power.
1709 Abraham Darby makes cast iron using coal as fuel, by coking the coal before putting it into the blast furnace.
1712 The Dudley Castle Newcomen, the first successful steam engine, is built.
1764 James Watt invents the separate condenser steam engine.
1769 Richard Arkwright invents a cotton-spinning machine.
1776 First commercial Watt engines built.
1783 First Watt double-acting rotative engine built. First manned flight in a *Montgolfier* balloon. Henry Cort invents the puddling process for making wrought iron.
1798 Eli Whitney contracts to make 10,000 muskets for the American government using interchangeable parts and mass-production methods.
1801 The Jacquard loom, first successful use of punched-card programming.

1802 Richard Trevethick patents "high-pressure" steam engines, small enough for railway engines.
1825 The Stockton and Darlington Railway, the first public railroad to use locomotives, is opened.
1831 Michael Faraday makes the key scientific discoveries which lay the foundation for electrical engineering.
1837 Babbage designs, but never builds, the first mechanical computer. Cooke and Wheatstone install an electrical telegraph.
1838 Morse code is first used.
1843 Ada Lovelace writes the first "computer programs" for Babbage's unbuilt mechanical computer.
1856 The Bessemer steelmaking process is announced.
1862 Louis Pasteur shows that germs cause disease. Gatling machine gun invented.
1876 Alexander Graham Bell invents the telephone.
1878/9 Joseph Swan and Thomas Edison invent electric light bulb.

The Rocket

1884 Charles Parsons invents steam turbine. The majority of modern power stations use steam turbines.

1885 Karl Benz builds one of the earliest automobiles.
1888 Thomas Boyd Dunlop invents the pneumatic tire.
1890 Forth railroad bridge, the first large steel structure, opens. City and South London Railway, the first electric tube railroad.
1895 X rays discovered by Röntgen.
1896 Guglielmo Marconi demonstrates his radio system to the British Post Office.
1897 First commercially successful diesel engine built.
1901 Marconi sends radio signals across the Atlantic.
1903 The Wright brothers make the first successful aircraft flight. Marie Curie is awarded the Nobel Prize (the first woman) or her work on radioactivity.
1904 John Ambrose Fleming invents the thermionic valve.
1905 Albert Einstein proposes the special theory of relativity.
1906 First experimental sound radio transmission.
1907 Bakelite, the first modern plastic, is invented.
1908 The Haber-Bosch process for making artificial nitrogen is invented. First Ford Model T car.

1915 Poison gas first used.
1916 Tanks first used, at the Battle of the Somme.

1919 First flight across the Atlantic, by Alcock and Brown in a *Vickers Vimy* bomber.
1920 First experimental public radio broadcasts.
1926 Aerosol cans invented by Eric Rotheim. First successful liquid-fuel rocket flight.
1927 First feature-length sound film, *The Jazz Singer*, released.
1930 Iconoscope electronic TV camera invented by Zworkin of RCA.
1931 Nylon invented by Wallace Carothers.
1933 Polyethylene discovered by ICI.
1935 Radar demonstrated by British scientists, led by Robert Watson-Watt.
1936 British public TV service starts.
1938 The ballpoint pen invented by the Biro brothers.
1940 Penicillin used.
1942 First nuclear reactor started in Chicago.
1944 First long-range rocket missile, Germany's V2, fired at London.
1945 First atomic bombs dropped on Japan.
1946 First electronic computer, the ENIAC.
1947 Polaroid cameras become available.

1948 Announcement of the invention of the transistor, by Shockley, Brattain, and Bardeen.

1952 United States explodes the first hydrogen bomb.
1953 Structure of DNA discovered by Crick and Watson. First trials of Salk's polio vaccine.
1954 Soviet Union builds the first nuclear power station.
1955 Oral contraceptive pill invented.
1956 Commercial reel-to-reel video tape systems introduced.
1957 The first satellite, *Sputnik 1*, is launched.
1959 Texas Instruments produces the first integrated circuits.
1960 The first laser and the first transistorized computers appear.
1961 Yuri Gagarin becomes the first man in space. Early industrial robots are produced.
1963 Audio cassette tapes become available for the first time.
1969 The first moon landing. Commercial video cassette systems become available. Global satellite communications network established.
1970 Bar code systems are invented by Monarch Marketing in America and Plessey in Britain.
1971 The first space station, *Salyut 1*, is launched. The first microprocessor, the *Intel 4004*, is produced.
1972 The laser-read video disk is invented but not perfected until 1978. The first brain scanner is produced.
1972 Commercial video games and pocket calculators available. Home video systems available.
1973 Body scanners.
1977 The *Apple II* personal computer is put on the market.

1978 The first test tube baby is born.
1979 The *Sony Walkman* personal stereo is produced.
1980 Compact disk audio systems appear. The *Unimation Puma* assembly robot is introduced.
1981 First space shuttle flight.

Ford Model T, 1908

1982 Martine Kempf invents the Katalavox miniature voice recognition system for operating microsurgery devices and wheelchairs.
1985 CD-ROM compact disk memory systems for computers are introduced.
1986 *Challenger* space shuttle explodes soon after takeoff. Chernobyl nuclear power station accident causes radioactive contamination.
1987 The Docklands Light Railway opens, Britain's first fully automatic system. Digital audio tape systems are introduced.
1990 Experimental live high-definition TV system broadcasts.
1991 Commercial virtual reality games introduced.

Space shuttle, 1980s

GLOSSARY

Airship A "lighter than air" flying machine which, unlike a balloon, has an engine and can be steered.

Alloy A mixture of different metals, or metals and other materials. It has different properties from the various ingredients. Examples are bronze, an alloy of copper and tin, and steel, an alloy of iron and carbon.

Antibiotic A drug that treats disease by destroying or injuring the harmful bacteria that carry it.

Astrolabe An early scientific instrument invented by the Greeks around 300 B.C. and used to measure the height of stars above the horizon.

Atomic bomb A bomb that gets its immense power from the fission (splitting) of atoms.

Automation Making machines that can work by themselves and do not need a human operator.

Biotechnology The use of living organisms to create products, manage the environment, or control industrial processes.

Blast furnace A furnace for smelting metal from ores into which air is blown to raise the heat.

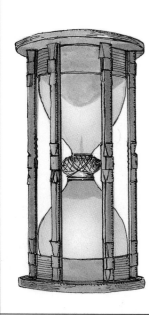

Calculator A mechanical or electronic machine used to formulate mathematical calculations.

Cast iron An alloy of iron and carbon which is hard but brittle. It cannot be forged, but can be melted and poured into molds to make complex shapes.

Cellular radio A network of small radio stations that give radio communication over a large area without any blank spots. Usually used for personal telephones.

Computer A machine (usually electronic) that can be programmed to carry out a complex series of mathematical calculations, or to control industrial or other processes.

DNA Deoxyribonucleic acid - the material that carries genetic information in living things and determines which individual characteristics are inherited.

Electronics Using or studying the movement of electrons; examples are radio and transistor technology and computer technology.

Four-stroke engine An internal combustion engine that produces power every fourth stroke. The full cycle is fuel intake stroke, compression, combustion (during which power is produced), and exhaust stroke.

Integrated circuit A piece of silicon or any other material from which transistors can be made, on which has been etched a large number of transistorized electronic circuits.

Internal combustion engine An engine that runs directly on the burning gases from its fuel. Examples are jet engines, diesel engines, and gas engines. An external combustion engine, like the steam turbine, runs off steam produced by burning fuel in a separate boiler.

Laser Light amplification by the stimulated emission of radiation. A device which produces a powerful, focused beam of light.

Lathe A machine that shapes objects by rotating them against a cutting tool. The lathe may have been invented about 2000 B.C.

Machine tool A tool that does not completely rely on the skill or strength of the user to shape an object.

Mass production Making a large number of identical objects usually by using machine tools.

Microprocessor A "silicon chip" which contains the central processing unit of a computer.

Optical fiber A thin glass fiber which can transmit light. Mainly used to carry laser beams for communication, or for surgery, or for inspecting things in confined spaces.

Patent The exclusive right to exploit an invention for a number of years, after which anyone can use it. The main conditions are that the invention must be new and unique, and that the inventor must publish a clear description of the invention.

Program A set of instructions controlling the operation of a computer or any other type of machine.

Radar Radio detecting and ranging - finding the position and speed of objects by bouncing radio waves off them and detecting the reflected waves. Used to detect aircraft and ships, as a navigational aid, or by spacecraft to map planets.

Radio Communication across long or short distances by sending signals using radio waves.

Robot A machine that mimics the action of a human being, or runs completely automatically.

Satellite Strict definition is a moon orbiting a planet, but is now more commonly used to mean any spacecraft orbiting the earth.

Silicon chip An integrated circuit made from silicon.

Steel An alloy of iron and carbon which can be forged, welded, or melted and cast into molds to make more complex shapes.

Steam turbine An engine that is driven by jets of steam passing through a series of blades that then turn a shaft.

Transistor A small electronic device which acts as a switch but which has no moving parts.

Vaccination Deliberately infecting someone with a mild form of a disease (usually by injection) to provide future immunity to that disease.

Virtual Reality Computer-controlled technology that allows the user to explore imaginary environments, such as buildings, that exist only as computer drawings.

Word processor A small computer which is capable of storing, editing, and manipulating text.

Wrought iron Almost pure iron; a soft metal which can be forged and welded but not cast.

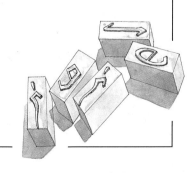

INDEX

PRINTED IN BELGIUM BY

INTERNATIONAL BOOK PRODUCTION